Digital Forensic Science

Issues, Methods, and Challenges

Synthesis Lectures on Information Security, Privacy, & Trust

Editor
Elisa Bertino, *Purdue University*
Ravi Sandhu, *University of Texas, San Antonio*

The Synthesis Lectures Series on Information Security, Privacy, and Trust publishes 50- to 100-page publications on topics pertaining to all aspects of the theory and practice of Information Security, Privacy, and Trust. The scope largely follows the purview of premier computer security research journals such as ACM Transactions on Information and System Security, IEEE Transactions on Dependable and Secure Computing and Journal of Cryptology, and premier research conferences, such as ACM CCS, ACM SACMAT, ACM AsiaCCS, ACM CODASPY, IEEE Security and Privacy, IEEE Computer Security Foundations, ACSAC, ESORICS, Crypto, EuroCrypt and AsiaCrypt. In addition to the research topics typically covered in such journals and conferences, the series also solicits lectures on legal, policy, social, business, and economic issues addressed to a technical audience of scientists and engineers. Lectures on significant industry developments by leading practitioners are also solicited.

Digital Forensic Science: Issues, Methods, and Challenges
Vassil Roussev

ISBN: 978-3-031-01223-5 paperback
ISBN: 978-3-031-02351-4 ebook

DOI 10.1007/978-3-031-02351-4

A Publication in the Morgan & Claypool Publishers series
SYNTHESIS LECTURES ON INFORMATION SECURITY, PRIVACY, & TRUST

Lecture #19
Series Editors: Elisa Bertino, *Purdue University*
              Ravi Sandhu, *University of Texas, San Antonio*
Series ISSN
Print 1945-9742   Electronic 1945-9750

Digital Forensic Science

Issues, Methods, and Challenges

Vassil Roussev
University of New Orleans

SYNTHESIS LECTURES ON INFORMATION SECURITY, PRIVACY, &
TRUST #19

ABSTRACT

Digital forensic science, or *digital forensics*, is the application of scientific tools and methods to identify, collect, and analyze digital (data) artifacts in support of legal proceedings. From a more technical perspective, it is the process of reconstructing the relevant sequence of events that have led to the currently observable state of a target IT system or (digital) artifacts.

Over the last three decades, the importance of digital evidence has grown in lockstep with the fast societal adoption of information technology, which has resulted in the continuous accumulation of data at an exponential rate. Simultaneously, there has been a rapid growth in network connectivity and the complexity of IT systems, leading to more complex behavior that needs to be investigated.

The goal of this book is to provide a systematic *technical* overview of digital forensic techniques, primarily from the point of view of computer science. This allows us to put the field in the broader perspective of a host of related areas and gain better insight into the computational challenges facing forensics, as well as draw inspiration for addressing them. This is needed as some of the challenges faced by digital forensics, such as cloud computing, require *qualitatively* different approaches; the sheer volume of data to be examined also requires new means of processing it.

KEYWORDS

digital forensics, cyber forensics, cyber crime, incident response, data recovery

To my parents, *Reni* and *Rosen*,
    for their love and for opening all of life's opportunities.

To my wife, *Laura*,
    for her love and unconditional support.

To my advisor, *Prasun*,
    for his patience and the enduring wisdom of his lessons.

Contents

CHAPTER 1

Introduction

> In a word, the computer scientist is a *toolsmith*—no more, but no less. It is an honorable calling.
>
> Frederick P. Brooks, Jr. [66]

Forensic science (or *forensics*) is dedicated to the systematic application of scientific methods to gather and analyze evidence for a legal purpose. *Digital forensics*—a.k.a. *cyber* or *computer* forensics—is a subfield within forensics, which deals specifically with digital artifacts, such as files, and computer systems and networks used to create, transform, transmit, and store them.

The rapid adoption of information technology (IT) in all aspects of modern life means that it bears witness to an ever expanding number of human- and machine-initiated interactions and transactions. It is increasingly the case that the *only* historical trace of such events exists in electronic form. At the same time, most IT systems are not *specifically* engineered to facilitate the forensic acquisition and analysis of their data. Therefore, there is the need to continuously develop forensic methods that keep up with the rapid growth in data volume and system complexity.

The main goal of this book is to provide a relatively brief, but systematic, *technical* overview of digital forensic methods, as they exist today, and to outline the main challenges that need to be addressed in the immediate future.

1.1   SCOPE OF THIS BOOK

By its nature, digital forensics is a multi-disciplinary undertaking, combining various expertise including software developers providing tools, investigators applying their analytical expertise, and lawyers framing the goals and bounds of the investigation. Nevertheless, the almost singular focus of this book is on the technical aspects of process—the algorithmic techniques used in the acquisition and analysis of the different systems and artifacts.

In other words, *the goal is to provide a computer science view of digital forensic methods*. This is in sync with Fred Brooks' thesis that the primary purpose of computer science research is to build computational tools to solve problems emanating from other domains: "Hitching our research to someone else's driving problems, and solving those problems on the owners' terms, leads us to richer computer science research." [66]

This means that we will only superficially touch upon the various legal concerns, or any of the issues regarding tool use, procedural training, and other important components of digital forensic practice. In part, this is due to the shortness of the book format, and the high quality coverage of these topics in existing literature.

However, the *primary* reason is that we seek to present digital forensics from a different perspective that has been missing. It is an effort to *systematize* the computational methods that we have acquired over the last three decades, and put them in a coherent and extensible framework.

Target audience.   The treatment of the topics is based on the author's experience as a computer science educator and researcher. It is likely to fit better as part of a special topics course in a general computer science curriculum rather than as part of a specialized training toward certification, or digital forensics degree.

We expect this text to be most appropriate in an advanced, or a graduate, course in digital forensics; it could also be used as supplemental material in an introductory course, as some of the topic treatment is different from other textbooks. We hope that faculty and graduate students will find it helpful as a starting point in their research efforts, and as a good reference on a variety of topics.

Non-goals.   It may be useful to point out explicitly what we are *not* trying to achieve. Broadly, we are not trying to replace any of the established texts. These come in two general categories:

- comprehensive introduction to the *profession* of the forensic investigator (often used as a primary textbook in introductory courses) such as Casey's *Digital Evidence and Computer Crime* [32];

- in-depth technical reference books on specialized topics of interest, such as Carrier's classic *File System Forensic Analysis* [23], *The Art of Memory Forensics* by Ligh et al. [108], or Carvey's go-to books on *Windows* [29] and registry analysis [30].

Due to the limitations of the series format, we have also chosen to forego a discussion on multimedia data and device forensics, which is a topic worth its own book, such as the one edited by Ho and Li [92].

1.2   ORGANIZATION

The book's structure is relatively flat with almost no dependencies among the chapters. The two exceptions are Chapter 3, which should be a prerequisite for any of the subsequent chapters, and Chapter 6, which will make most sense as the closing discussion.

Chapter 2 provides a brief history of digital forensics, with an emphasis on technology trends that have driven forensic development. The purpose is to supply a historical context for the methods and tools that have emerged, and to allow us to reason about current challenges, and near-term developments.

Chapter 3 looks at the digital forensics process from several different perspectives—legal, procedural, technical, and cognitive—in an effort to provide a full picture of the field. Later, these models are referenced to provide a framework to reason about a variety of challenges, from managing data volumes to improving the user interface of forensic tools.

Chapter 4 is focused on *system* forensics; that is, on the types of evidentiary artifacts that are produced during the normal operation of computer systems. Most of these are operating system and application data structures, but we also discuss the emerging problem of cloud system forensics.

Chapter 5 discusses *artifact* forensics: the analysis of autonomous data objects, usually files, that have self-contained representation and meaningful intepretation outside the scope of a specific computer system. These include text, images, audio, video, and a wide variety of composite document formats.

Chapter 6 is an effort to outline a medium-term research agenda that is emerging from the broader trends in IT, such as fast data growth, cloud computing, and IoT. The focus is on the difficult problems that need to be addressed in the next five years rather than on the specific engineering concerns of today, such as finding ways to get around encryption mechanisms.

CHAPTER 2

Brief History

The beginning of the modern era of digital forensics can be dated to the mid-1980s, which saw the adoption of 18 U.S.C. § 1030 [1] as part of the *Comprehensive Crime Control Act of 1984* [33]. The *Computer Fraud and Abuse Act* of 1986 was enacted by the U.S. Congress as the first of several amendements to clarify and expand the scope of the provisions. In 1984, the FBI initiatated its *Magnetic Media Program* [72], which can be viewed as a watershed moment in recognizing the importance of digital evidence, and the need for professionalization of the field.

Prior to that, computer professionals used ad-hoc methods and tools primarily for the purposes of data extraction and recovery after unforeseen failures and human errors; to this day, data recovery remains a cornerstone of digital forensic methodology. In the pre-1984 days, there was little effort to build a systematic body of knowledge, or specialized expertise. This is not surprising as there was little societal need—computers were centralized timeshare systems used by businesses, and had little useful information for the legal system. This all began to change with the massive surge in popularity of personal computers, and the introduction of dial-up networking for consumers.

2.1 EARLY YEARS (1984–1996)

The following dozen years (1984–1996) saw a rapid increase in personal computer use, along with fast growth in private network services like *CompuServe*, *Prodigy*, and *AOL*. This exploration period is characterized by substantial diversity of hardware and software, and saw the emergence of early *de facto* standard file formats (e.g., GIF [45]), most of which were poorly documented and rarely formally described [72].

Toward the end of the period, the meteoric rise in popularity of the *Netscape Navigator* web browser marked the tipping point for the transition to standards-based internetworking. At the same time, the combination of the *Intel x86* architecture and *Microsoft Windows* operating system became the dominant software on the PC desktop. Taken together, these developments rapidly reduced the platform diversity and enabled a coherent view of the digital forensic process to gradually emerge. It also became feasible to become an expert by focusing on just one platform that (at the time) had minimal security and privacy provisions to impede the analysis. For example, one of the major forensic vendors today, *AccessData*, advertised itself as "leaders in cryptography and password recovery since 1987," and offered a set of tools for that purpose [2].

In other words, the main uses of the forensic techniques of the time was to provide locksmith and disaster recovery services. Accordingly, the main thrust of the efforts was reverse-engineering/brute-forcing of the (weak) application-level encryption techniques employed by various vendors, and filesystem "undelete," which enabled the (partial) recovery of ostensibly deleted information.

2.2   GOLDEN AGE (1997–2007)

Around 1997, we saw the emergence of the first commercial tools, like *EnCase Forensic*, that specifically targeted law enforcement use cases and provided an integrated environment for managing a case. This marked the beginning of a decade (1997–2007) of rapid expansion of forensic capabilities, both commercial and open source, against a backdrop of growing use of the Internet for business transactions, and a relatively weak understanding and use of privacy and security mechanisms. Garfinkel refers to this period as a "Golden Age" of digital forensics [72]. During this time, we saw the establishment of the first academic conference—*DFRWS* (dfrws.org) in 2001—with the exclusive focus on basic and applied digital forensic research.

The most important source of forensic data during the period became local storage in the form of internal HDDs and removable media—CD/DVD and USB-attached flash/disk drives. This reflects an IT environment in which most computations were performed on workstations by standalone applications. Although the importance of the Internet was increasing dramatically, most of the related evidence could still be found in the local email client, or (web) browser caches. Thus, filesystem analysis and reconstruction (Section 4.1.4) became the main focus of forensic tools and investigations, and Carrier's definitive book on the subject [23] can be seen as a symbol of the age.

At the time, RAM was not considered a worthy source of evidence and there were no analytical tools beyond `grep` and `hexdump` to make sense of it. This began to change in 2005 with the first *DFRWS* memory forensics challenge [53], which led to the development of a number of tools for *Microsoft Windows* (discussed in Section 4.2); a follow-up challenge [76] focused research efforts on developing *Linux* memory analysis tools.

Between 2004 and 2007 several technology developments hinted that a new chapter in the history of the field was getting started. In 2004, *Google* announced the *Gmail* service [79]; its main significance is to show that a web application can be deployed on an Internet scale. Web apps are an implementation of the *software as a service* (SaaS) delivery model in which the client device needs no application-specific installation locally; most of the computation is performed on the provider's server infrastructure and only a small amount of user interface (UI) code is downloaded on the fly to manage the interaction with the user. Forensically, this is a big shift as most of the artifacts of interest are resident on the *server* side.

In 2006, Amazon announced its public cloud service [3], which greatly democratized access to large-scale computational resources. It suddenly became possible for *any* web app—not just the ones from companies with big IT infrastructure—to work at scale; there was no conceptual impediment for all software vendors to go the SaaS route. In practice, it took several years for this movement to become mainstream but, with the benefit of hindsight, it is easy to identify this as a critical moment in IT development.

In 2007, it was *Apple*'s turn to announce a major technology development—the first *smartphone* [6]; this was quickly followed by a Google-led effort to build a competing device using open source code, and the first *Android* device was announced in 2008 [183]. Mobile computing had been around for decades, but the smartphone combined a pocket-portable form factor with general purpose compute platform and ubiquitous network communication, to become—in less than a decade—the indispensible daily companion for the vast majority of people. Accordingly, it has become a witness of their actions, and a major source of forensic evidence.

2.3   PRESENT (2007–)

The current period is likely to be viewed as transitional. On the one hand, we have very mature techniques for analyzing persistent storage (Section 4.1) and main memory (Section 4.2) for all three of the main operating systems (OS) for the desktop/server environments—*Microsoft Windows*, *MacOS*, and *Linux*. Similarly, there are well-developed forensic tools for analyzing the two main mobile OS environments—*Android* and *iOS*.

On the other hand, we see exponential growth in the volume of forensic data in need of processing (Section 6.1) and the accelerating transition to cloud-centric IT (Section 4.6). As our discussion will show, the latter presents a qualitatively new target and requires a new set of tools to be developed. Separately, we are also seeing a maturing use of security and privacy techniques, such as encryption and media sanitization, that eliminate some traditional sources of evidence, and make access to others problematic.

It is difficult to predict what will be the event(s) that will mark the logical beginning of the next period, but one early candidate is the announcement of the *AWS Lambda* platform [9]. There is a broad consensus that the next major technology shift (over the next 10–15 years) will be the widespread adoption of the *Internet of Things* (IoT) [7]. It is expected that it will bring online between 10 and 100 times more Internet-connected devices of all kinds. The fast growing adoption of *AWS Lambda* as a means of working with these devices suggests that it could have a similar impact on the IT landscape to that of the original introduction of *AWS*.

Lambda provides a platform, in which customers write event-handling functions that require no explicit provisioning of resources. In a typical workflow, a device uploads a piece of data to a storage service, like *AWS S3*. This triggers an event, which is automatically dispatched to an instance of a user-defined handler; the result may be the generation of a series of subsequent events in a processing pipeline. From a forensic perspective, such an IT model renders existing techniques obsolete, as there is no meaningful data to be extracted from the embedded device itself.

2.4   SUMMARY

The main point of this brief walk through the history of digital forensics is to link the predominant forensic methods to the predominant IT environment. Almost all techniques in widespread use today are predicated on access to the full environment in which the relevant computations were performed. This started with standalone personal computers, which first became connected to the network, then became mobile, and eventually became portable and universally connected. Although each step introduced incremental challenges, the overall approach continued to work well.

However, IT is undergoing a rapid and dramatic shift from using software *products* to employing software *services*. Unlike prior developments, this one has *major* forensic implications; in simple terms, tools no longer have access to the full compute environment of the forensic target, which is a service hosted somewhere in a shared data center. Complicating things further is the fact that most computations are ephemeral (and do not leave the customary traces) and storage devices are routinely sanitized.

We will return to this discussion in several places throughout the text, especially in Chapter 6. For now, the main takeaway is that the future of forensics is likely to be different than its past and present. That being said, the bulk of the content will naturally focus on systematizing what we already know, but we will also point out the new challenges that may require completely new solutions.

CHAPTER 3

Definitions and Models

Forensic science is the application of scientific methods to collect, preserve, and analyze evidence related to legal cases. Historically, this involved the systematic analysis of (samples of) *physical* material in order to establish causal relationships among various events, as well as to address issues of provenance and authenticity.[1] The rationale behind it—*Locard's exchange principle*—is that physical contact between objects inevitably results in the exchange of matter leaving *traces* that can be analyzed to (partially) reconstruct the event.

With the introduction of digital computing and communication, the same general assumptions were taken to the cyber world, largely unchallenged. Although a detailed conceptual discussion is outside the intent of this text, we should note that the presence of *persistent* "digital traces" (broadly defined) is neither inevitable nor is it a "natural" consequence of the processing and communication of digital information. Such records of cyber interactions are the result of concious engineering decisions, ones not usually taken *specifically* for forensic purposes. This is a point we will return to shortly, as we work toward a definition that is more directly applicable to *digital* forensics.

3.1 THE DAUBERT STANDARD

Any discussion on forensic evidence must inevitably begin with the *Daubert* standard—a reference to three landmark decisions by the Supreme Court of the United States: *Daubert v. Merrell Dow Pharmaceuticals*, 509 U.S. 579 (1993); *General Electric Co. v. Joiner*, 522 U.S. 136 (1997); and *Kumho Tire Co. v. Carmichael*, 526 U.S. 137 (1999).

In the words of Goodstein [78]: "The presentation of scientific evidence in a court of law is a kind of shotgun marriage between the two disciplines. ... The *Daubert* decision is an attempt (not the first, of course) to regulate that encounter."

These cases set a new standard for expert testimony [11], overhauling the previous *Frye* standard of 1923 (*Frye v. United States*, 293 F. 1013, D.C. Cir. 1923). In brief, the Supreme Court instructed trial judges to become gatekeepers of expert testimony, and gave four basic criteria to evaluate the admissability of forensic evidence:

1. The theoretical underpinnings of the methods must yield testable predictions by means of which the theory could be falsified.

2. The methods should preferably be published in a peer-reviewed journal.

---

[1]A more detailed definition and discussion of traditional forensics is beyond our scope.

3. There should be a known rate of error that can be used in evaluating the results.

4. The methods should be generally accepted within the relevant scientific community.

The court also emphasized that these standards are flexible and that the trial judge has a lot of leeway in determining admissability of forensic evidence and expert witness testimony. During legal proceedings, special *Daubert* hearings are often held in which the judge rules on the admissibility of expert witness testimony requested by the two sides.

In other words, scientific evidence becomes *forensic* only if the court deems it admissible. It is a somewhat paradoxic situation that an evaluation of the scientific merits of a specific method is rendered by a judge, not scientists. There is no guarantee that the legal decision, especially in the short term, will be in agreement with the ultimate scientific consensus on the subject. The courts have a tendency to be conservative and skeptical with respect to new types of forensic evidence. The admissability decision also depends on the specific case, the skill of the lawyers on both sides, the communication skills of the expert witnesses, and a host of other factors that have nothing to do with scientific merit.

The focus of this book is on the scientific aspect of the analytical methods and, therefore, we develop a more technical definition of *digital forensic science*.

3.2   DIGIAL FORENSIC SCIENCE DEFINITIONS

Early applications of digital forensic science emerged out of law enforcement agencies, and were initiated by investigators with *some* technical background, but no formal training as computer scientists. Through the 1990s, with the introduction and mass adoption of the Internet, the amount of data and the complexity of the systems investigated grew quickly. In response, digital forensic methods developed in an ad hoc, on-demand fashion, with no overarching methodology, or peer-reviewed venues. By the late 1990s, coordinated efforts emerged to formally define and organize the discipline, and to spell out best field practices in search, seizure, storage, and processing of digital evidence [126].

3.2.1   LAW-CENTRIC DEFINITIONS

In 2001, the first *Digital Research Forensic Workshop* was organized with the recognition that the ad hoc approach to digital evidence needed to be replaced by a systematic, multi-disciplinary effort to firmly establish digital forensic science as a rigorous discipline. The workshop produced an in-depth report outlining a research agenda and provided one of the most frequently cited definitions of *digital forensic science* [136]:

> **Digital forensics**: The use of scientifically derived and proven methods toward the preservation, collection, validation, identification, analysis, interpretation, documentation, and presentation of digital evidence derived from digital sources for the purpose of facilitating or furthering the reconstruction of events found to be criminal, or helping to anticipate unauthorized actions shown to be disruptive to planned operations.

This definition, although primarily stressing the investigation of criminal actions, also includes an anticipatory element, which is typical of the notion of forensics in operational environments. The analysis there is performed primarily to identify the vector of attack and scope of a security incident; identifying adversary with any level of certainty is rare, and prosecution is not the typical outcome.

In contrast, the reference definition provided by NIST a few years later [100] is focused entirely on the legal aspects of forensics, and emphasizes the importance of strict chain of custody:

> **Digital forensics** is considered the application of science to the identification, collection, examination, and analysis of data while preserving the integrity of the information and maintaining a strict chain of custody for the data. Data refers to distinct pieces of digital information that have been formatted in a specific way.

Another way to describe these law-centric definitions is that they provide a litmus test for determining whether specific investigative tools and techniques qualify as being *forensic*. From a legal perspective, this open-ended definition is normal and works well as the admissability of all evidence gets decided during the legal proceedings.

From the point of view of a technical discussion, however, such definitions are too generic to provide a meaningful starting point. Further, the chain of custody issues are primarily of procedural nature and do not bring up any notable technical problems. Since the goal of this book is to consider the technical aspects of digital forensics, it would be prudent to start with a working definition that is more directly related to our subject.

3.2.2 WORKING TECHNICAL DEFINITION

We adopt the working definition first introduced in [154], which directly relates to the formal definition of computing in terms of *Turing* machines, and is in the spirit of Carrier's computer history model (Section 3.3.2):

> **Digital forensics** is the process of reconstructing the relevant sequence of events that have led to the currently observable state of a target IT system or (digital) artifacts.

Notes

1. The notion of *relevance* is inherently case-specific, and a big part of a forensic analyst's expertise is the ability to identify case-relevant evidence.

2. Frequently, a critical component of the forensic analysis is the causal attribution of event sequence to specific human actors of the system (such as users and administrators).

3. The provenance, reliability, and integrity of the data used as evidence are of primary importance.

We view all efforts to perform system, or artifact, analysis after the fact as a form of forensics. This includes common activities, such as incident response and internal investigations, which almost never result in any legal actions. On balance, only a tiny fraction of forensic analyses make it to the courtroom as formal evidence; this should not constrain us from exploring the full spectrum of techniques for reconstructing the past of digital artifacts.

The benefit of employing a broader view of forensic computing is that it helps us to identify closely related tools and methods that can be adapted and incorporated into forensics.

3.3   MODELS OF FORENSIC ANALYSIS

In this section we discuss three models of the forensic analysis; each considers a different aspect of the analysis and uses different methods to describe the process. Garfinkel's *differential analysis* (Section 3.3.1) approach formalizes a common logical inference technique (similar, for example, to differential diagnosis in medicine) for the case of computer systems. In this context, diffential analysis is an incremental technique to reason about the likely prior state and/or subsequent events of individual artifacts (e.g., a file has been copied).

Carrier's *computer history model* (Section 3.3.2) takes a deeper mathematical approach in describing forensics by viewing the computer system under investigation as a *finite state machine*. Although it has few *direct* practical implications, it is a conceptually important model for the field. Some background in formal mathematical reasoning is needed to fully appreciate its contribution.

The final model of Pirolli and Card (Section 3.3.3) does not come from the digital forensics literature, but from cognitive studies performed on intelligence analysts. It is included because we believe that the analytical process is *very* similar and requires the same type of skills. Understanding how analysts perform the cognitive tasks is of critical importance to designing usable tools for the practice. It also helps in understanding and modeling the differences in the level of abstraction at which the three groups of experts—forensic researchers/developers, analysts, and lawyers—operate.

3.3.1   DIFFERENTIAL ANALYSIS

The vast majority of existing forensic techniques can be described as special cases of *differential analysis*—the comparison of two objects, *A* and *B*, in order to identify the differences between them. The ultimate goal is to infer the sequence of events that (likely) have transformed A into B (A preceeds B in time). In the context of *digital* forensics, this fundamental concept has only recently been formalized by Garfinkel et al. [75], and the rest of this section introduces the formal framework they put forward.

Terminology

Historically, differencing tools (such as the venerable *diff*) have been applied to a wide variety of artifacts, especially text and program code, long before they were employed for forensic use. The following definitions are introduced to formally generalize the process.

- *Image.* A byte stream from any data-carrying device representing the object under analysis. This includes all common evidence sources—disk/filesystem images, memory images, network captures, etc.

  Images can be *physical*, or *logical*. The former reflect (at least partially) the physical layout of the data on the data store. The latter consists of a collection of self-contained objects (such as files) along with the logical relationships among them without any reference to their physical storage layout.

- *Baseline image, A.* The image first acquired at time T_A.

- *Final image, B.* The last acquired image, taken at time T_B.

- *Intermediary images, I_n.* Zero, or more, images recorded between the baseline and final images; I_n is the nth image acquired.

- *Common baseline* is a single image that is a common ancestor to multiple final images.

- *Image delta, $B - A$,* is the differences between two images, typically between the baseline image and the final image.

- The *differencing strategy* defines the rules for identifying and reporting the differences between two, or more, images.

- *Feature, f,* is a piece of data that is either directly extracted from the image (file name/size), or is computed from the content (crypto hash).

- *Feature in image, (A, f).* Features are found in images; in this case, feature f is found in image A.

- *Feature name, NAME (A, f).* Every feature may have zero, one, or multiple names. For example, for a *file content* feature, we could use any of the file names and aliases under which it may be known in the host filesystem.

- *Feature location,* $Loc(f)$, describes the address ranges from which the content of the particular feature can be extracted. The locations may be either physical, or logical, depending on the type of image acquired.

- A *feature extraction function,* $F()$, performs the extraction/computation of a feature based on its location and content.

- *Feature set,* $F(A)$, consists of the features extracted from an image A, using the extraction function $F()$.

- The *feature set delta,* $F(B) - F(A)$, contains the differences between the feature sets extracted from two images; the delta is not necessarily symmetric.

- *Transformation sequence,* R, consists of the sequence of operations that, when applied to A, produce B. For example, the Unix *diff* program can generate a *patch file* that can be used to transform a text file in this fashion. In general, R is not unique and there can be an infinite number of transformations that can turn A into B.

Generalized Differential Analysis

As per [75], each feature has three pieces of metadata:

Location: A mandatory attribute describing the address of the feature; each feature must have at least one location associated with it. *Name*: A human-readable identifier for the feature; this is an optional attribute. *Timestamp(s) and other metadata*: Features may have one, or more, timestamps associated with them, such as times of creation, modification, last access, etc. In many cases, other pieces of metadata (key-value pairs) are also present.

Given this framework, differential analysis is performed *not* on the data images A and B, but on their corresponding feature sets, $F(A)$ and $F(B)$. The goal is to identify the operations which transform $F(A)$ into $F(B)$. These are termed *change primitives*, and seek to explain/reproduce the feature set changes.

In the general case, such changes are not unique as the observation points may fail to reflect the effects of individual operations which are subsequently overridden (e.g., any access to a file will override the value of the last access time attribute). A simple set of change inference rules is defined (Table 3.1) and formalized (Table 3.2) in order to bring consistency to the process. The rules are *correct* in that they transform $F(A)$ into $F(B)$ but do not necessarily describe the actual operations that took place. This is a fundamental handicap for any differential method; however, in the absence of complete operational history, it is the best that can be accomplished.

If A and B are from the same system and $T_A < T_B$, it would appear that all *new* features in the feature set delta $F(B) - F(A)$ should be timestamped after T_A. In other words, if B were to contain features that predate T_A, or postdate T_B, then this would rightfully be considered an inconsistecy. An investigation should detect such anomalies and provide a sound explanation

Table 3.1: Change detection rules in plain English ([75], Table 1)

If something did not exist and now it does, it was created
If it is in a new location, it was moved
If it did exist before and now it does not, it was deleted
If more copies of it exist, it was copied
If fewer copies of it exist, something got deleted
Aliasing means names can be added or deleted

Table 3.2: Abstract rules for transforming $A \rightarrow B$ (A into B) based on observed changes to features, f, feature locations Loc (A, f), and feature names Name (A, f). Note: The Rename primitive is not strictly needed (as it can be modeled as AddName followed by DelName), but it is useful to convey higher-level semantics ([75], Table 2).

Rule	Change Primitive for $A \underset{R}{\rightarrow} B$
$f \in F(A) \land f \in F(B)$	(No change)
$f \notin F(A) \land f \in F(B)$	Create f
$f \in F(A) \land f \notin F(B)$	Delete f
$\|Loc(A,f)\| = 1 \land \|Loc(A,f)\| = 1 \land$ Loc$(A,f) \neq$ Loc(B,f)	Move Loc$(A,f) \rightarrow$ Loc(B,f)
$\|Loc(A,f)\| < \|Loc(B,f)\|$	Copy Loc $(A,f) \rightarrow ($Loc$(B,f) \mid$ Loc $(A,f))$
$\|Loc(A,f)\| > \|Loc(B,f)\|$	Delete (Loc $(A,f) \mid$ Loc$(B,f))$
$\|Name(A,f)\| = 1 \land \|Name(B,f)\| = 1 \land$ Name$(A,f) \neq$ Name(B,f)	Rename Name$(A,f) \rightarrow$ Loc(B,f)
$(\|Name(A,f)\| \neq 1 \lor \|Name(B,f)\| \neq 1) \lor$ $(n \notin Name(A,f) \land n \in Name(B,f))$	AddName f, n
$(\|Name(A,f)\| \neq 1 \lor \|Name(B,f)\| \neq 1) \lor$ $(n \in Name(A,f) \land n \notin Name(B,f))$	DelName f, n

based on knowledge of how the target system operates. There is a range of possible explanations, such as:

Tampering. This is the easiest and most obvious explanation although it is not necessarily the most likely one; common examples include planting of new files with old timestamps, and system clock manipulation.

System operation. The *full* effects of the underlying operation, even as simple as copying a file, are not always obvious and require careful consideration. For example, the Unix *cp* command sets the creation time of the new copy to the time of the operation but will keep the original modification time if the *-p* option is used.

Time tracking errors. It has been shown [127, 167] that operating systems can introduce inconsitencies during normal operation due to rounding and implementation errors. It is worth noting that, in many cases, the accuracy of a recorded timestamp is of little importance to the operation of the system; therefore, perfection should not be assumed blindly.

Tool error is always a possibility; like all software, forensic tools have bugs and these can manifest themselves in unexpected ways.

One important practical concern is how to *report* the extracted feature changes. Performing a comprehensive differential analysis, for example, of two hard disk snapshots is likely to result in an enormous number of individual results that can overwhelm the investigator. It is critical that differencing tools provide the means to improve the quality and relevance of the results. This can be accomplished in a number of ways: (a) *filtering* of irrelevant information; (b) *aggregation* of the results to highlight both the common and the exceptional cases; (c) *progressive disclosure* of information, where users can start at the aggregate level and use queries and hierchies to drill down to the needed level of detail; (d) *timelining*—provide a chronological ordering of the (relevant) events.

3.3.2   COMPUTER HISTORY MODEL

Differential analysis offers a relatively simple view of forensic inference, by focusing on the beginning and end state of the data, and by expressing the difference in terms of a very small set of primitive operations. The *computer history model* (CHM) [27]—one of Carrier's important contributions to the field—seeks to offer a more detailed and formal description of the process. The model employs finite state machines to capture the state of the system, as well as its (algorithmic) reaction to outside events. One of the main considerations is the development of an investigative model that avoids human bias by focusing on modeling the computation itself along with strict scientific hypothesis testing. The investigation is defined as a series of yes/no questions (predicates) that are evaluated with respect to the available history of the computation.

Primitive Computer History Model

This assumes that the computer being investigated can be represented as a *finite state machine* (FSM), which transitions from one state to another in reaction to events. Formally, the FSM is a quintuple $(Q, \Sigma, \delta, s0, F)$, where Q is a finite set of states, Σ is a finite alphabet of event symbols, δ is the transition function $\delta : Q \times \Sigma \rightarrow Q$, $s0 \in Q$ is the starting state of the machine, and $F \subseteq Q$ is the set of final states.

The *primitive history* of a system describes the lowest-level state transitions (such as the execution of individual instructions), and consists of the sequence of primitive states and events that occurred.

The *primitive state* of a system is defined by the discrete values of its primitive, uniquely addressable storage locations. These may include anything from a CPU register to the content of network traffic (which is treated as temporary storage). As an illustration, Figure 3.1 shows an event E_1 reading the values from storage locations R_3 and R_6 and writing to locations R_3 and R_4.

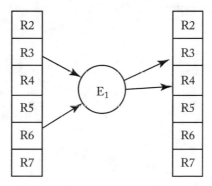

Figure 3.1: Primitive computer history model example: event E_1 is reading the values from storage locations R_3 and R_6 and writing to locations R_3 and R_4 [27].

The *primitive history* is the set T containing the times for which the system has a history. The duration between each time in T, Δt, must be shorter than the fastest state change in the system. The *primitive state history* is function $h_{ps} : T \to Q$ that maps a time $t \in T$ to the primitive state that existed at that time. The *primitive event history* is a function $h_{pe} : T \to \Sigma$ that maps a time $t \in T$ to a primitive event in the period $(t - \Delta t, t + \Delta t)$.

The model described so far is capable of describing a static computer system; in practice, this is insufficient as a modern computing system is dynamic—it can add resources (such as storage) and capabilities (code) on the fly. Therefore, the computer history model uses a dynamic FSM model with sets and functions to represent the changing system capabilities. Formally, each of the Q, Σ, and δ sets and functions can change for each $t \in T$.

Complex Computer History Model

The primitive model presented is rarely practical on contemporary computer systems executing billions of instructions per second (code reverse engineering would be an exceptional case). Also, there is a mismatch between the level of abstraction of the representation and that of the questions that an investigator would want to ask (e.g., *was this file downloaded?*). Therefore, the model provides the means to aggregate the state of the system and ask questions at the appropriate level of abstraction.

Complex events are state transitions that cause one or more lower-level complex or primitive events to occur; for example, copying a file triggers a large number of primitive events. *Complex storage locations* are virtual storage locations created by software; these are the ephemeral and persistent data structures used by software during normal execution. For example, a file is a complex storage location and the name value attribute pairs include the file name, several different timestamps, permissions, and content.

Figure 3.2 shows a complex event E_1 reading from complex storage locations D_1 and D_2 and writing a value to D_1. At a lower level, E_1 is performed using events E_{1a} and E_{1b}, such as CPU, or I/O instructions. The contents of D_1 and D_2 are stored in locations (D_{1a}, D_{1b}) and (D_{2a}, D_{2b}), respectively.

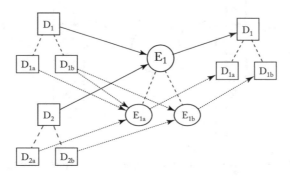

Figure 3.2: Complex history event examples: event E_1 with two complex cause locations and one complex effect location [27].

General Investigation Process

The sequence of queries pursued by the investigator will depend on the specific objectives of the inquiry, as well as the experience and training of the person performing it. The CHM is agnostic with respect to the overall process followed (we will discuss the cognitive perspective in Section 3.3.3) and does not assume a specific sequence of high-level phases. It does, however, postulate that the inquiry follow the general scientific method, which typically consists of four phases: *Observation*, *Hypothesis Formulation*, *Prediction*, and *Testing & Searching*.

Observation includes the running of appropriate tools to capture and observe aspects of the state of the system that are of interest, such as listing of files/processes, and rendering the content of files. During *Hypothesis Formulation* the investigators use the observed data, and combine it with their domain knowledge to formulate hypothesis that can be tested, and potentially falsified, in the history model. In the *Prediction* phase, the analyst identifies specific evidence that would be consistent, or would be in contradiction, with the hypothesis. Based on the predictions, experiments are performed in the *Testing* phase, and the outcomes are used to guide further iterations of the process.

Categories of Forensic Analysis

Based on the outlined framework, the CHM identifies seven categories of analytical techniques.

History duration.   The sole techniques in this category and is *operational reconstruction*—it uses event reconstruction and temporal data from the storage devices to determine when events occurred and at what points in time the system was active. Primary sources for this analysis include log files, as well as the variety of timestamp attributes kept by the operating system and applications.

Primitive storage system configuration.   The techniques in this category define the capabilities of the primitive storage system. These include the names of the storage devices, the number of addresses for each storage device, the domain of each address on each storage device, and when each storage device was connected. Together, these sets and functions define the set of possible states Q of the FSM.

Primitive event system configuration.   Methods in this category define the capabilities of the primitive event system; that is, define the names of the event devices connected, the event symbols for each event device, the state change function for each event device, and when each event device was connected. Together, these sets and functions define the set of event symbols Σ and state change function δ. Since primitive events are almost never of direct interest to an investigation, these techniques are not generally performed.

Primitive state and event definition.   Methods in this category define the primitive state history (h_{ps}) and event history (h_{es}) functions. There are five types of techniques that can be used to formulate and test this type of hypothesis and each class has a directional component. Since different approaches can be used to defining the *same* two functions, a hypothesis can be formulated using one technique and tested with another. Overall, these are impractical in real investigations, but are presented below for completeness.

Observation methods use direct observation of an output device to define its state in the inferred history, and are only applicable to output device controllers; they cannot work for internal devices, such as hard disks.

Capabilities techniques employ the primitive system capabilities to formulate and test state and event hypotheses. To formulate a hypothesis, the investigator chooses a possible state or event at random; this is impractical for almost all real systems as the state space is enormous.

Sample data techniques extract samples from observations of similar systems or from previous executions of the system being investigated; the results are metrics on the occurrence of events and states. To build a hypothesis, states and events are chosen based on how likely they are to occur. Testing the hypothesis reveals if there is evidence to support the state or event. Note that this is a conceptual class not used in practice as there are no relevant sample data.

Reconstruction techniques use a known state to formulate and test hypotheses about the event and state that existed immediately prior to the known state. This is not performed in practice, as questions are rarely formulated about primitive events.

Construction methods are the forward-looking techniques that use a known state to formulate and test hypotheses about the next event and state. This is not useful in practice as the typical starting point is an end state; further, any hypothesis about the future state would not be testable.

Complex storage system configuration.   Techniques in this category define the complex storage capabilities of the system, and are needed to formulate and test hypotheses about complex states. The techniques define the names of the complex storage types (D_{cs}), the attribute names for each complex storage type (DAT_{cs}), the domain of each attribute (ADO_{cs}), the set of identifiers for the possible instances of each complex storage type (DAD_{cs}), the abstraction transformation functions for each complex storage type (ABS_{cs}), the materialization transformation functions for each complex storage type (MAT_{cs}), and the complex storage types that existed at each time and at each abstraction layer $X \in L$ (c_{cs-X}).

Two types of hypotheses are formulated in this category: the first one defines the names of the complex storage types and the states at which they existed; the second defines the attributes, domains, and transformation functions for each complex storage type. As discussed earlier, complex storage locations are program data structures. Consequently, to enumerate the complex storage types in existance at a particular point in time requires the reconstruction of the state of the computer, so that program state could be analyzed.

Identification of existing programs can be accomplished in one of two ways: *program identification*—by searching for programs on the system to be subsequently analyzed; and *data type observation*—by inferring the presence of complex storage types that existed based on the data types that are found. This latter technique may give false positives in that a complex type may have been created elsewhere and transferred to the system under investigation.

Three classes of techniques can be used to define the attributes, domains, and transformation functions for each complex storage type: (a) *complex storage specification observation*, which uses a specification to define a program's complex storage types; (b) *complex storage reverse engineering*, which uses design recovery reverse engineering to define complex storage locations; (c) *complex storage program analysis*, which uses static, or dynamic, code analysis of the programs to identify the instructions creating, or accessing, the complex storage locations and to infer their structure.

It is both impractical and unnecessary to fully enumerate the data structures used by programs; only a set of the most relevant and most frequently used ones are supported by investigative tools, and the identification process is part of the tool development process.

Complex event system configuration.   These methods define the capabilities of the complex event system: the names of the *programs* that existed on the system (D_{ce}), the names of the *abstraction layers* (L), the symbols for the *complex events* in each program (DSY_{ce-X}), the *state change* functions for the complex events (DCG_{ce-X}), the *abstraction transformation* functions (ABS_{ce}), the *materialization transformation* functions (MAT_{ce}), and the *set of programs* that existed at each time (c_{ce}).

Inferences about events are more difficult than those about storage locations because the latter are both abstracted and materialized and tend to be long-lived because of backward compatibility; the former are usually designed from the top-down, and backward compatibility is a much lesser concern.

Three types of hypotheses can be tested in this category: (a) programs existence, including period of their existence; (b) abstraction layers, event symbols, and state change functions for each program; (c) the materialization and abstraction transformation functions between the layers.

With respect to (a), both *program identification* and *data type reconstruction* can be used in the forms already described.

For hypotheses in regard to (b), there are two relevant techniques—*complex event specification observation* and *complex event program analysis*. The former uses a specification of the program to determine the complex events that it could cause. The latter works directly with the program to observe the events; depending on the depth of the analysis, this could be as simple as running the program under specific circumstances, or it could be a massive reverse engineering effort, if a (near-)complete picture is needed.

The hypotheses in part (c) concern the rules defining the mappings between higher-level and lower-level events. Identifying these rules is an inherently difficult task, and Carrier proposed only one type of technique with very limited applicability—*development tool and process analysis*. It analyzes the programming tools and development process to determine how complex events are defined.

Complex state and event definition. This category of techniques defines the complex states that existed (h_{cs}) and the complex events that occurred (h_{ce}). It includes eight classes of analysis techniques and each has a directional component (Figure 3.3). Two concern individual states and events, two are forward- and backward-based, and four are upward- and downward-based.

Complex state and event system capabilities methods use the capabilities of the complex system to formulate and test state and event hypotheses based on what is possible. The main utility of this approach is that it can show that another hypothesis is impossible because it is outside of the system's capabilities.

Complex state and event sample data techniques use sample data from observations of similar systems or from previous executions. The results include metrics on the occurrence of events and states and would show which states and events are most likely. This class of techniques is employed in practice in an ad hoc manner; for example, if a desktop computer is part of the investigation, an analyst would have a hypothesis about what type of content might be present.

Complex state and event reconstruction methods use a state to formulate and test hypotheses about the previous complex event and state. This approach is frequently employed, although the objective is rarely to reconstruct the state *immediately* preceeding a known one, but an earlier

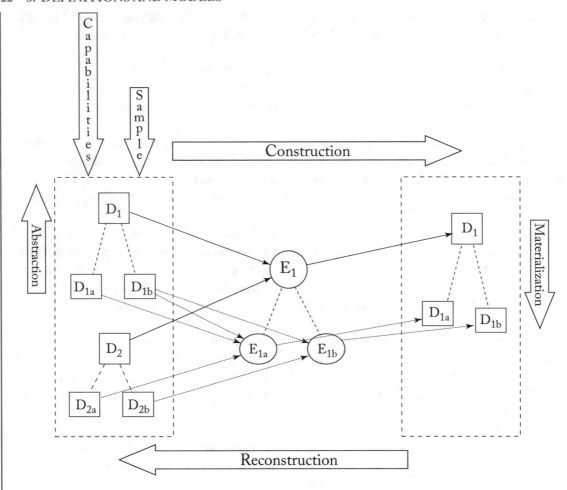

Figure 3.3: The classes of analysis techniques for defining complex states and events have directional components to them. [27].

one. Common examples include analyzing web browser history, or *most recently used* records to determine what the user has recently done.

Complex state and event construction techniques use a known state to formulate and test hypotheses about the next event and state. Similarly to the corresponding techniques at the primitive level, complex-level construction techniques are rarely used to define the event and the *immediately* following state. Instead, they are employed to predict what events *may* have occurred. For example, the content of a user document, or an installed program, can be the basis for a hypothesis on what other events and states may have occured afterward.

The final four classes of methods either *abstract* low-level data and events to higher-level ones, or perform the reverse—*materialize* higher-level data and events to lower levels. *Data abstraction* is a bottom-up approach to define complex storage locations (data structures) using lower-level data and data abstraction transformation rules. For example, given a disk volume, we can use knowledge about the filesystem layout to transform the volume into a set of files.

Data materialization is the reverse of data abstraction, transforming higher-level storage locations into lower-level ones using materialization rules, and has limited practical applications.

Event abstraction is the bottom-up approach to define complex events based on a sequence of lower-level events and abstraction rules. This has limited applicability to practice because low-level events tend to be too many to log; however, they can be used in the process of analyzing program behavior.

Event materialization techniques are the reverse of event abstraction, where high-level events and materialization rules are used to formulate and test hypotheses about lower-level complex and primitive events. For example, if a user is believed to have performed a certain action, then the presence, or absence, of lower-level traces of their action can confirm, or disprove, the hypothesis.

3.3.3   COGNITIVE TASK MODEL

The differential analysis technique presented in Section 3.3.1 is a basic building block of the investigative process, one that is applied at varying levels of abstraction and to a wide variety of artifacts. However, it does not provide an overall view of how forensic experts actually perform an investigation. This is particularly important in order to build forensic tools that properly support the cognitive processes.

Unfortunately, digital forensics has not been the subject of any serious interest from cognitive scientists and there have been no coherent efforts to document forensic investigations. Therefore, we adopt the sense-making process originally developed by Pirolli and Card [142] to describe intelligence analysis—a cognitive task that is very similar to forensic analysis. The Pirolli–Card cognitive model is derived from an in-depth *cognitive task analysis* (CTA), and provides a reasonably detailed view of the different aspects of an intelligence analyst's work. Although many of the tools are different, forensic and intelligence analysis are very similar in nature—in both cases analysts have to go through a mountain of raw data to identify (relatively few) relevant facts and put them together in a coherent story. The benefit of using this model is that: (a) it provides a fairly accurate description of the investigative process in its own right, and allows us to map the various tools to the different phases of the investigation; (b) it provides a suitable framework for explaining the relationships of the various models developed within the area of digital forensics; and (c) it can seamlessly incorporate into the investigation information from other sources.

The overall process is shown in Figure 3.4. The rectangular boxes represent different stages in the information-processing pipeline, starting with raw data and ending with presentable results. Arrows indicate transformational processes that move information from one box to another.

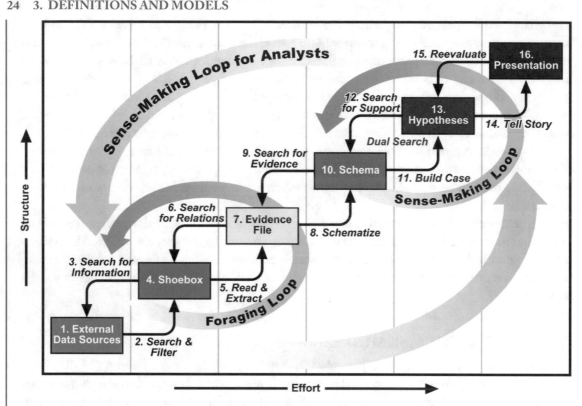

Figure 3.4: Notional model of sense-making loop for analysts derived from cognitive task analysis [185, p. 44].

The *x* axis approximates the overall level of effort to move information from raw to the specific processing stage. The *y* axis shows the amount of structure (with respect to the investigative process) in the processed information for every stage. Thus, the overall trend is to move the relevant information from the lower left to the upper right corner of the diagram. In reality, the processing can both meander through multiple iterations of local loops and jump over phases (for routine cases handled by an experienced investigator).

External data sources include all potential evidence sources for the specific investigation, such as disk images, memory snapshots, network captures, as well as reference databases, such as hashes of known files. The *shoebox* is a subset of all the data that has been identified as potentially relevant, such as all the email communication between two persons of interest. At any given time, the contents of the shoebox can be viewed as the analyst's approximation of the information content potentially relevant to the case. The *evidence file* contains only the parts that directly speak to the case, such as specific email exchanges on topics of interest.

The *schema* contains a more organized version of the evidence, such as a timeline of events, or a graph of relationships, which allows higher-level reasoning over the evidence. A *hypothesis* is a tentative conclusion that explains the observed evidence in the schema and, by extension, could form the final conclusion. Once the analyst is satisfied that the hypothesis is supported by the evidence, the hypothesis turns into a *presentation*, which is the final product of the process. The presentation usually takes on the form of an investigator's report that both speaks to the high-level conclusions relevant to the legal case, and also documents the low-level technical steps based on which the conclusion has been formed.

The overall analytical process is split into two main activity loops: a *foraging loop* that involves actions taken to find potential sources of information, query them, and filter them for relevance; and a *sense-making loop* in which the analyst develops—in an iterative fashion—a conceptual model that is supported by the evidence. The information transformation processes in the two loops can be classified into bottom-up (organizing data to build a theory) or top-down (finding data based on a theory). In practice, analysts apply these in an opportunistic fashion with many iterations.

Bottom-up Processes

Bottom-up processes are synthetic—they build higher-level (more abstract) representations of the information from more specific pieces of evidence.

- *Search and filter*: External data sources, hard disks, network traffic, etc., are searched for relevant data based on keywords, time constraints, and others in an effort to eliminate the vast majority of the data that are irrelevant.

- *Read and extract*: Collections in the shoebox are analyzed to extract individual facts and relationships that can support or disprove a theory. The resulting pieces of artifacts (e.g., individual email messages) are usually annotated with their relevance to the case.

- *Schematize*: At this step, individual facts and simple implications are organized into a schema that can help organize and help identify the significance and relationship among a growing number of facts and events. Timeline analysis is one of the basic tools of the trade; however, any method of organizing and visualizing the facts—graphs, charts, etc.—can greatly speed up the analysis. This is not an easy process to formalize, and most forensic tools do not directly support it. Therefore, the resulting schemas may exist on a piece of paper, on a whiteboard, or only in the mind of the investigator. Since the overall case could be quite complicated, individual schemas may cover only specific aspects of it, such as the sequence of events discovered.

- *Build case*: Out of the analysis of the schemas, the analyst eventually comes up with testable theories that can explain the evidence. A theory is a tentative conclusion and often requires more supporting evidence, as well as testing against alternative explanations.

- *Tell story*: The typical result of a forensic investigation is a final report and, perhaps, an oral presentation in court. The actual presentation may only contain the part of the story that is strongly supported by the digital evidence; weaker points may be established by drawing on evidence from other sources.

Top-down Processes

Top-down processes are analytical—they provide context and direction for the analysis of less structured data search and organization of the evidence. Partial, or tentative conclusions, are used to drive the search of supporting and contradictory pieces of evidence.

- *Re-evaluate*: Feedback from clients may necessitate re-evaluations, such as the collection of stronger evidence, or the pursuit of alternative theories.

- *Search for support*: A hypothesis may need more facts to be of interest and, ideally, would be tested against all (reasonably) possible alternative explanations.

- *Search for evidence*: Analysis of theories may require the re-evaluation of evidence to ascertain its significance/provenance, or may trigger the search for more/better evidence.

- *Search for relations*: Pieces of evidence in the file can suggest new searches for facts and relations on the data.

- *Search for information*: The feedback loop from any of the higher levels can ultimately cascade into a search for additional information; this may include new sources, or the re-examination of information that was filtered out during previous passes.

Foraging Loop

It has been observed [138] that analysts tend to start with a high-recall/low-selectivity query, which encompassed a fairly large set of documents—many more than the analyst can afford to read. The original set is then successively modified and narrowed down before the documents are read and analyzed.

The *foraging loop* is a balancing act between three kinds of processing that an analyst can perform—*explore*, *enrich*, and *exploit*. Exploration effectively expands the shoebox by including larger amounts of data; enrichment shrinks it by providing more specific queries that include fewer objects for consideration; exploitation is the careful reading and analysis of an artifact to extract facts and inferences. Each of these options has varying cost and potential rewards and, according to information foraging theory [141], analysts seek to optimize their cost/benefit trade-off.

Sense-making Loop

Sense-making is a cognitive term and, according to Klein's [102] widely quoted definition, is the ability to make sense of an ambiguous situation. It is the process of creating situational awareness and understanding to support decision making under uncertainty; it involves the understanding of connections among people, places, and events in order to anticipate their trajectories and act effectively.

There are three main processes that are involved in the sense-making loop: *problem structuring*—the creation and exploration of hypotheses, *evidentiary reasoning*—the employment of evidence to support/disprove hypothesis, and *decision making*—selecting a course of action from a set of available alternatives.

Data Extraction vs. Analysis vs. Legal Interpretation

Considering the overall process from Figure 3.4, we gain a better understanding of the relationships among the different actors. At present, forensics researchers and tool developers primarily provide the means to extract data from the forensic targets (step 1), and the basic means to search and filter it. Although some data analytics and natural language processing methods (like entity extraction) are starting to appear in dedicated forensic software, these capabilities are still fairly rudimentary in terms of their ability to automate parts of the sense-making loop.

The role of the legal experts is to support the upper right corner of the process in terms of building/disproving legal theories. Thus, the investigator's task can be described as the translation of highly specific technical facts into a higher-level representation and theory that explains them. The explanation is almost always tied to the sequence of actions of humans involved in the case.

In sum, investigators need not be software engineers but must have enough proficiency to understand the significance of the artifacts extracted from the data sources, and be able to competently read the relevant technical literature (peer-reviewed articles). Similarly, analysts must have a working understanding of the legal landscape and must be able to produce a competent report, and properly present their findings on the witness stand, if necessary.

CHAPTER 4

System Analysis

Modern computer systems in general use still follow the original *von Neumann* architecture [192], which models a computer system as consisting of three main functional units—CPU, main memory, and secondary storage—connected via data buses. This chapter explores the means by which forensic analysis is applied to these subsystems. To be precise, the actual investigative targets are the respective operating system modules controlling the different hardware subsystems.

System analysis is one of the cornerstones of digital forensics. The average user has very little understanding of what kind of information operating systems maintain about their activities, and frequently do not have the knowledge and/or privilege level to tamper with system records. In effect, this creates a "Locard world" where their actions leave a variety of traces that allow their actions to be tracked.

System analysis provides insight with a lot of leverage and high pay-offs in that, once an extraction, or analytical method, is developed, it can be directly applied to artifacts created by different applications.

4.1 STORAGE FORENSICS

Persistent storage in the form of hard disk drives (HDDs), solid state drives (SSDs), optical disks, external (USB-connected) media, etc., is the primary source of evidence for most digital forensic investigations. Although the importance of memory forensics in solving cases has grown tremendously, a thorough examination of persistent data has remained a critical component of almost all forensic investigations since the very beginning.

4.1.1 DATA ABSTRACTION LAYERS

Computer systems organize raw storage in successive layers of abstraction—each software layer (some may be in firmware) builds incrementally more abstract data representations dependent only on the interface provided by the layer immediately below it. Accordingly, forensic storage analysis can be performed at several levels of abstraction:

Physical media. At the lowest level, every storage device encodes a sequence of bits and it is, in principle, possible to use a custom mechanism to extract the data bit by bit. In practice, this is rarely done, as it is an expensive and time-consuming process. One example of this process are second-generation mobile phones for which it is feasible to physically remove (desolder) the memory chips and perform acquisition of the content [194]. Thus, the lowest level at which most practical examinations are performed is the *host bus adapter* (HBA) interface. Adapters implement a standard protocol (SATA, SCSI, etc.) through which they can be made to perform low-level operations. For damaged hard drives, it is often possible to perform at least partial forensic repair and data recovery [123]. In all cases, the goal of the process is to obtain a copy of the data in the storage device for further analysis.

Block device. The typical HBA presents a block device abstraction—the medium is presented as a sequence of fixed-size blocks, commonly of 512 or 4,096 bytes, and the contents of each block can be read or written using block read/write commands. The media can be divided into partitions, or multiple media may be presented as a single logical entity (e.g., RAIDs). The typical data acquisition process works at the block device level to obtain a working copy of the forensic target— a process known as *imaging*—on which all further processing is performed.

Filesystem. The block device has no notion of files, directories, or—in most cases—which blocks are considered used and which ones are free; it is the filesystem's task to organize the block storage into file-based storage in which applications can create files and directories with all of their relevant attributes—name, size, owner, timestamps, access permissions, and others. For that purpose, the filesystem maintains metadata, in addition to the contents of user files.

Application artifacts. User applications use the filesystem to store various artifacts that are of value to the end-user—documents, images, messages, etc. The operating system itself also uses the file system to store its own image—executable binaries, libraries, configuration and log files, registry entries—and to install applications. Some application artifacts, such as compound documents, can have a complex internal structure integrating multiple data objects of different types.

Analysis of application artifacts tends to yield the most immediately relevant results as the recorded information most directly relates to actions and communications initiated by humans. As the analysis goes deeper (to a lower level of abstraction), it requires greater effort to independently reconstruct the actions of the system. For example, by understanding the on-disk structures of a specific filesystem, a tool can reconstruct a file out of its constituent blocks. Such knowledge is particularly costly to obtain from a closed system, such as *Microsoft Windows*, because of the substantial amount of blackbox reverse engineering effort involved.

Despite the cost, independent forensic reconstruction is of critical importance for several reasons:

(a) it enables the recovery of evidentiary data that is not available through the normal data access interface;

(b) it forms the basis for recovering partially overwritten data; and

(c) it allows the discovery and analysis of malware agents that have subverted the normal functioning the system, making data obtained via the regular interface untrustworthy.

4.1.2   DATA ACQUISITION

In line with best practices [100], analysis of data at rest is not carried out on a live system. The target machine is powered down, an exact bit-wise copy of the storage media is created, the original is stored in an evidence locker, and all forensic work is performed on the copy. There are exceptions to this workflow in cases where it is not practical to shut down the target system and, therefore, a media image is obtained while the system is live. Evidently, such an approach does not provide the same level of consistency guarantees, but can still yield valuable insight. The issue of consistency does not exist in virtualized environments, where a consistent image of the virtual disk can be trivially obtained by using the built-in snapshot mechanism.

As already discussed, obtaining the data from the lowest-level system interface available, and independently reconstructing higher-level artifacts, is considered the most reliable approach to forensic analysis. This results in strong preference for acquiring data at lower levels of abstraction and the concepts of *physical* and *logical* acquisition.

> **Physical data acquisition** is the process of obtaining the data *directly* from the hardware media, without the mediation of any (untrusted) third-party software.

An example of this approach is Willassen's discussion [194] of cell phone data acquisition that relies on removing the physical memory chip and reading the data directly from it. More generally, getting physical with the evidence source is something most practical and necessary for low-end embedded systems with limited hardware capabilities.

For general-purpose systems, tools use an HBA protocol, such as *SATA*, or *SCSI*, to interrogate the storage device and obtain a copy of the data. The resulting image is a *block-level* copy of the target and the process is usually referred to as physical acquisition by most investigators; Casey uses the more accurate term *pseudo-physical* to account for the fact that not all areas of the physical media are acquired.

It is worth noting that modern storage controllers are quickly evolving into autonomous storage devices, which implement complex (proprietary) wear-leveling and load-balancing algorithms. This has two major implications: (a) the numbering of data blocks becomes decoupled from actual physical location; and (b) it is increasingly possible that the storage controller itself becomes compromised [196], rendering the acquisition process untrustworthy. These caveats notwithstanding, *we will refer to block-level acquisition as physical*, in line with accepted terminology.

> **Logical data acquisition** relies on one, or more, software layers as intermediaries to acquire the data from the storage device.

In other words, the tool uses an API, or a message protocol, to perform the task. The integrity of this method hinges on the correctness and the integrity of the implementation of the

API, or protocol. In addition to the risk, however, there is also a reward—higher-level interfaces present a data view that is closer in abstraction to that of user actions and application data structures. Experienced investigators (equipped with the proper tools) make use of both physical and logical views to obtain and verify the evidence relevant to the case.

HBA firmware compromises. It is important to realize that, although not trivial to execute, attacks on the integrity of the disk controller have been shown to be entirely feasible. For example, early experiments by Goodspeed [77] showed how an iPod can be customized (with relative ease) to detect the read patterns of an acquisition process, and to react by hiding and destroying the data on the fly.

In follow up work, Zaddach et al. [196] reverse engineered from scratch a *Seagate* disk controller and installed a backdoor, allowing a remote attacker to "mount" the disk and examine its content. This involves no compromises to the software stack above the firmware.

We bring up these examples to underscore the fact that *any* reliance on a software layer introduces the potential for compromise. Therefore, adequate measures to ensure the trustworthiness of the software stack must be taken to ensure the integrity of the evidence. In current practice, this is an issue that is largely ignored, and the trustworthiness of the firmware is taken for granted.

Block-level acquisition can be accomplished in software, hardware, or a combination of both. The workhorse of forensic imaging has been the `dd` Unix/Linux general purpose command-line utility [68], which can produce a binary copy of any file, device partition, or an entire storage device. For example, the command `dd if=/dev/sda1 of=target.dd`, would produce a binary copy of the first partition of the first SCSI/SATA drive and will place it in the file named `target.dd`.

A hardware write blocker is often installed on the target device to eliminate the possibility of operator or tool error that leads to the accidental modification of the target. Further, cryptographic hashes are computed for the entire image and (optionally) for every block. The latter can be used to demonstrate the integrity of the evidence in case the original device suffers a partial failure, which makes it impossible to read its entire contents. To simplify the acquisition process, more specialized versions of `dd`, such as `dcfldd` [87] and `dc3dd` [104], provide additional functionality, such as on-the-fly hashing and integrity verification, multiple output streams, and detailed logging.

Ddrescue [67] is another variation on `dd`, which automatically tries to recover from read errors over multiple runs in an effort to extract as much data as possible from a failing hard drive. It is another example of a system administration tool that was designed to deal with recovery from disk failures but can also be immediately incorporated into a forensic case.

Virtually all commercial forensic tools, as well as a number of other open source projects, provide the basic disk imaging capability. There are also specialized hardware devices for duplicating drives (e.g., [83]). Under the hood, they utilize open source tools but also add a simplified interaction model that reduces the probability of errors; this can be particularly valuable in streamlining the operation of a forensic lab.

The National Institute of Justice (NIST) maintains the Computer Forensic Tool Testing (CFTT) project [128], which independently tests various basic tools, such as write blockers [130] and image acquisition tools [129], and regularly publishes reports on its findings.

4.1.3   FORENSIC IMAGE FORMATS

Forensic image formats describe the syntax and semantics of the output of imaging tools, and enable the acquisition of the data to be decoupled from its analysis.

Raw.   The simplest one is the *raw* image, which corresponds to a bit-wise identical copy of all the blocks on the target in sequential order. Since this is the output from the dd tool, this format is sometimes referred to as the *dd* format. It is the lowest common denominator, and is ingested by all forensic tools capable of working directly with disk/volume images (as opposed to individual files). The clear advantage of the raw format is that it is the simplest possible, and the data is ready for immediate processing.

From a forensic standpoint, a raw image—by itself—is insufficient. Additional metadata identifying essential attributes (case number, computer system, hardware model, method of acquisition, chain of custody, etc.) must accompany the image both for operational and archival purposes. As well, a cryptographic hash of the whole image must be present, at a minimum, to provide the means for integrity verification.

Preferably, additional hashes at the block level should also be present to allow the identification of partially corrupted data. One particular problem that the raw format cannot solve is how to encode blocks that were unreadable due to media corruption. Tools will usually fill such blocks with zeroes, however, this is not a proper solution as it makes the block indistinguishable from uncorrupted blocks consisting of zeroes. It is also highly desirable to have a format that integrates compression, and allows targeted extraction of specific blocks (without decompressing the whole image). To address these challenges, a number of forensic image formats have been put forward, of which we discuss the two most consequential ones.

EnCase (EWF/E01).   The *Expert Witness Compressed Format* (EWF) [152] was originally introduced by *ASR Data* as the evidence container format for the *SMART* application. EWF, *aka* the *E01* format (after the extension used for the image file), has been widely adopted by commercial forensic tools, such as *EnCase Forensic* and *FTK*, and has become the *de facto* industry standard. Version 2 of the format was introduced in 2012 [84] and contains a number of new features, including support for encryption.

Most open source tools support *EWF* format via the `libewf` library [120] developed by Metz, who maintains a public working draft of specifications of the formats [118, 119]. The brief description here follows the working draft terminology and narrative.

The original EWF (Figure 4.1) has a simple structure consisting of a *file header* containing basic case metadata, and a series of zip-compressed data blocks (RFC 1950, 1951). There are *Adler 32* checksums covering the header and each of the data blocks, as well as an MD5 message digest of the whole file. Although EWF is a workable format in widespread use, it has a number of shortcomings, such as: lack of facilities to indicate corrupted data blocks, no native means to represent logical acquisitions, difficulty in gaining selective access to the data, and no facilities to sign and encrypt the content.

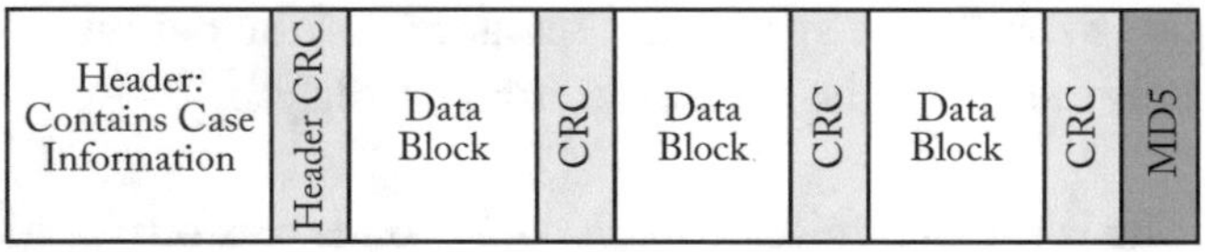

Figure 4.1: Structure of the Expert Witness Format (version 1).

An updated version of the format, referred to as *EWF2*, or *Ex01*, was introduced in order to address some of these deficiencies by supporting: (a) AES-based data encryption; (b) second compression algorithm (bzip2); (c) out-of-order block ordering; (d) efficient representation of constant-pattern blocks; (e) data structure enhancements to improve performance.

The overall EWF2 structure (Figure 4.2) consists of a sequence of segments. Each segment consists of a fixed length header, followed by a sequence of *Link* data structures (or *sections* per [118]). Sections consist of a *LinkData* component, containing a chunk of raw data, and a *LinkRecord* providing a description of the data: *type/tag*—indicates the data type: device information, case data, sector data, etc.; *data flags*—indicates whether the data is hashed and/or encrypted; *previous section offset*—provides the position relative to the start of the segment file of the *previous* section; *data size, (MD5) integrity hash*; *(Adler-32) checksum*.

One notable change from EWF is that the section descriptor is at the end of the section and the section descriptor points to its previous section. Thus, the proper way to read the sections is from back to front.

AFF. The first version of *advanced forensic format* (AFF) was put forward by Garfinkel et al. [73] in 2006 (well before EWF2) with the aim of providing a robust, open source storage format that can be extended to accommodate future needs. An explicit goal was to supply a robust library under permissive license to allow vendors to support the format with minimal investment. The AFF design splits the data into two layers: *disk-representation* and *data-representation*. The former defines a scheme for storing disk images (along with relevant metadata), whereas the latter maps AFF segments to a file layout. For the sake of brevity, we omit a more detailed discussion of the original AFF; instead, we focus on the updated AFF4 version.

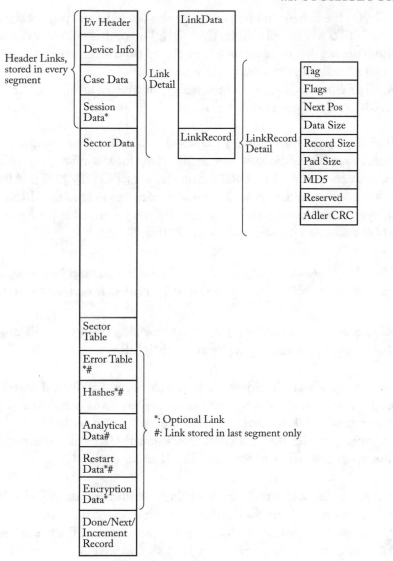

Figure 4.2: Structure of the Expert Witness Format (version 2) [84].

Although the AFF format never changed, there were three releases of the associated set of tools (`afflib`). Therefore, AFF4 is considered the fourth version of AFF, and it is a complete redesign based on the observed *limitations of AFF*: (a) inability to store multiple device images (belonging to the same case) in a single file; (b) limited metadata model restricted to simple key-value pairs; (c) inability to store memory and network captures; (d) no means for storing extracted files, or hyperlinks; (e) the encryption system leaks information about the contents of an evidence file; (f) the default compression page size (16 MB) can impose significant overhead when accessing NTFS Master File Tables (MFT); (g) no central directory of the contents of the file. It was also observed that there is much to be gained from adopting a container format already in wide use, and no real gain from using a custom one.

AFF4 [41] follows an object-oriented design, in which a small number of generic objects are presented with externally accessible behavior:

- The *AFF Object* is the basic building block and each instance has a unique name. Specifically, AFF4 uses a scheme of globally unique identifiers for identifying and referring to all data objects, and defines the AFF4 URN scheme (as per RFC 1737 [177]). All names belong to the `aff4` namepsace and begin with the prefix string `urn:aff4`. The URNs are made unique by employing a *universally unique identifier* (UUID) generated as per RFC 4122 [106]; e.g., `urn:aff4:bcc02ea5-eeb3-40ce-90cf-7315daf2505e`.

- A *Relation* is a *(Subject, Attribute, Value)* tuple and is a relationship between two AFF Objects, or between an object and a property. All metadata is represented in this manner.

- An *Evidence Volume* is a type of AFF Object providing storage to AFF segments. Volumes allow for storing and retrieving segments by their URN.

  Directory volume. This is the simplest type of volume, which stores different segments based on their URNs in a single directory. Since some filesystems (e.g., Microsoft Windows) are unable to represent URNs directly, URNs are encoded according to RFC 1738 [12]. The `aff4:stored` provides the base URL, and segment URLs are constructed by appending the escaped segment URN to the base URL (Listing 4.1:[2–3]).

  Zip64 volume. The default volume container file format for AFF4 is the widely used Zip64 [143] format. A *zip* file consists of a sequence of file records, each of which has a *local file header*, *(compressed) file data*, and a *data description*. The header holds a number of file attributes, such as name, timestamps, and size, as well as the version and compression method information. The data descriptor provides a CRC32 checksum and the compressed and uncompressed sizes.

  One particularly useful feature of the format is the *central directory*, which is placed at the very end. This allows for easy addition of files (only one seek) and easy transmission as a stream.

  Although Zip64 supports multi-file archives, and has extensions for encryption and authentications, due to the specific requirements of forensic containers, AFF4 provides its own custom implementations of these functions.

Listing 4.1: Example properties files for several AFF4 objects (some URNs shortened) [41]

```
1 Directory Volume :
2   urn:aff4:f901be8e-d4b2 aff4:stored=http://../case1/
3   urn:aff4:f901be8e-d4b2 aff4:type=directory
4 ZipFile Volume:
5   urn:aff4:98 a6dad6-4918 aff4:stored=file:///file.zip
6   urn:aff4:98 a6dad6-4918 aff4:type=zip
7 Image Stream:
8   urn:aff4:83 a3d6db-85 d5 aff4:stored=urn:aff4:f901be8e-d4b2
9   urn:aff4:83 a3d6db-85 d5 aff4:chunk_size=32k
10  urn:aff4:83 a3d6db-85 d5 aff4:chunks_in_segment=256
11  urn:aff4:83 a3d6db-85 d5 aff4:type=image
12  urn:aff4:83 a3d6db-85 d5 aff4:size=5242880
13 Map Stream:
14  urn:aff4:ed8f1e7a-94 aa aff4:target_period=3
15  urn:aff4:ed8f1e7a-94 aa aff4:image_period=6
16  urn:aff4:ed8f1e7a-94 aa aff4:blocksize=64k
17  urn:aff4:ed8f1e7a-94 aa aff4:stored=urn:aff4:83 a3d6db-85d5
18  urn:aff4:ed8f1e7a-94 aa aff4:type=map
19  urn:aff4:ed8f1e7a-94 aa aff4:size=0xA00000
20 Link Object:
21  map aff4:target=urn:aff4:ed8f1e7a-94aa
22  map aff4:type=link
23 Identity Object:
24  urn:aff4:identity/41:13 aff4:common_name=/C=US/ST=CA
25                  /L= SanFrancisco/O=Fort-Funston/CN=client1
26                  /emailAddress=me@myhost.mydomain
27  urn:aff4:identity/41:13 aff4:type=identity
28  urn:aff4:identity/41:13 aff4:statement=00000000
29  urn:aff4:identity/41:13 aff4:x509=urn:aff4:identity/41:13/cert.pem
30 Statement:
31  urn:aff4:34 a62f06/00000 aff4:sha256=+Xf4i..7rPCgo=
32  urn:aff4:34 a62f06/00000.idx aff4:sha256=ptV7xOK6..C7R6Xs=
33  urn:aff4:34 a62f06/properties aff4:sha256=yoZ..YMtk=
34  urn:aff4:34 a62f06 aff4:sha256=udajC5C.BVii7psU=
```

- A *Stream* is a type of AFF Object providing the ability to provide random access to a chunk of data, by means of a POSIX-like `open`/`seek`/`read`/`write` API; it also has a *size* attribute indicating the last addressable byte of the stream.

  Image streams. An image stream tagged with an `aff4:type` attribute value of *image*, and stores a single read-only forensic data set. Most frequently, the data is a storage device (HDD/SSD/USB) image, RAM snapshot, or network traffic capture.

The data is organized as a collection of data segments, called *bevies*, and each is stored in a separate volume. Segment URNs are generated by appending an eight-digit, zero-padded decimal integer representation of an incrementing id to the stream URN (e.g., urn:aff4:83a3d6db-85d5/00000032).

A *bevy* consists of a sequence of zlib-compressed chunks, preceded by a chunk index, which provides the offset for each one of them (Figure 4.3). The chunk index segment URN is derived by appending .idx to the bevy URN. Image stream attributes specify the chunk size and the number of chunks per segment (Listing 4.1:[9–10]).

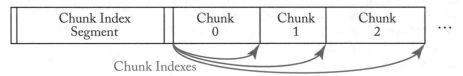

Figure 4.3: Structure of an image stream *bevy*: Each is a collection of compressed chunks stored back to back. Relative chunk offsets are stored in the chunk index segment [41].

Map streams. Map streams provide a linear transformation function which maps the logical offset of a data object to its physical storage in the container. For example, it may provide the location of the constituent blocks for a file, the mapping between virtual pages to memory frames, or the packets comprising a TCP session. AFF4 also provides efficient means to specify periodic mapping relationships like those needed during the reconstruction of RAID arrays (Listing 4.1:[14–19]).

HTTP streams. HTTP URLs are directly supported by AFF4 and can be used to both read and write (via WebDav) data. HTTP streams also support other common network protocols like FTP and HTTPS protocols, as provided by libcurl [179].

Encrypted streams. The need for specialized encryption streams is motivated by the fact that, although the Zip64 standard provides encryption facilities, it does not support PKI, or PGP. The *encrypted stream* provides transparent encryption and decryption onto a single target stream. The actual encrypted data is stored in the *target* stream; the encryption serves as a translation layer, which satisfies the I/O requests and transparently encrypts/decrypts the data on the fly.

The link object is an aliasing mechanism that allows for short, human-friendly names to be assigned to targets (Listing 4.1:[21–22]).

The identity object represents an entity, described in the notation of an X.509 certificate (Listing 4.1:[24–29]). Identity objects contain aff4:statement attributes which refer to AFF4 streams containing statements.

Statements is a collection of relations, or *(object, attribute, value)* tuples. For example, Listing 4.1:[31–34] defines (base64-encoded [96]) SHA256 digests for four different objects.

- A *Segment* is a single unit of data written to a volume, and has an URN, timestamp, and content. Segments present a stream interface and are intended for storing small amounts of data.

- A *Reference* provides the means to refer to objects by a Uniform Resource Identifier (URI). The URI can be another AFF Object URN or may be a more general Uniform Resource Locator (URL), such as a HTTP object. References allow objects to refer to other objects in different volumes, and facilitate more expressive and efficient data representation.

- The *Resolver* is a central data store which collects and resolves all attributes belonging to AFF Objects.

In sum, AFF4 comes closest to an accepted open source standard. It was designed with simplicity and extensibility in mind, and subsequent work has demonstrated its practical use in large-scale incident response and forensics [50] and has been extended to meet additional needs [175].

4.1.4   FILESYSTEM ANALYSIS

The typical storage device presents a *block device* interface with B_{max} number of blocks of size B_{size}. All read and write I/O operations are executed at the granularity of a whole block.[1] Historically, with rare exceptions, the standard block size adopted by HDD manufacturers has been 512 bytes. With the 2011 introduction of the *Advanced Format* standard [180], storage devices can support larger blocks, with 4,096 bytes being the preferred new size.

Regardless of the base block size, many operating systems manage storage in *clusters*; *a cluster is a contiguous sequence of blocks and is the smallest unit at which raw storage is allocated/reclaimed*. Thus, the block/sector size advertised by the drive may be 4KiB, but—if the cluster size is 16KiB—the OS will allocate them in groups of four.

For administration purposes, the raw drive is split into one, or more, contiguous areas called *partitions*. The idea is that each partition has a designated use and can be independently manipulated. Partitions can further be organized into *volumes*. A physical volume maps to an individual partition, whereas a *logical volume* can integrate multiple partitions from potentially multiple devices. This could be done in a RAID [35] configuration (for performance/reliability reasons), or as a concatenation of partitions presenting a single device with the cummulative capacity. In sum, volumes present a block device interface that allows for the decoupling of the physical media organization from the logical view presented to the operating system.

Although some volumes/partitions may be left raw (for later/specialized use), almost all are formatted to accommodate a particular file system (or *filesystem*). The purpose of the filesystem is

---

[1]In the context of HDDs, the term *sector* is used with the same meaning. However, in view of the broad diversification of storage technologies, we use the more general term "block" throughout the text.

to organize and maintain the on-device data structures that permit the persistent storage of user file content and related metadata. The filesystem is part of the operating system and presents an API, which allows applications to create, modify, and delete files; it also allows the grouping of files into a hierarchical structure of *directories* (or *folders*).

> A **file** is a named (opaque) sequence of bytes stored persistently.

As a general rule, the format and interpretation of the file content is almost always outside the purview of the operating system; it is the concern of relevant applications acting on behalf of users.

> A **file system** (*filesystem*) is an OS subsystem responsible for the persistent storage and organization of user and system files.

It provides a high-level API used by applications to store and retrieve files by name without concern for the physical storage method employed, or the layout of the data (and metadata) content.

> **Filesystem forensics** uses knowledge of the filesystem data structures, and the algorithms used to create, maintain, and delete them to:
> (a) extract data content from devices independently of the operating system instance which created it; and
> (b) extract leftover artifacts to which the regular filesystem API does not offer access.

The first feature is important to ensure that the data is not being modified during acquisition, and that any potential security compromises (of the target) do not affect the validity of the data. The second one can provide access to (parts of) deallocated files that have not been overwritten, purposely hidden data, and an implied history of filesystem operation—creation/deletion of files—that is not explicitly maintained by the OS.

Persistent storage has two autonomous layers of management, one at the block device level, and a second one at the filesystem level. These can be viewed as coarse- and fine-grained storage management, respectively.

Block Device Analysis

Before the OS can organize a filesystem on a raw device, it needs to be split into a set of one, or more, disjoint *partitions*.

> A block device **partition**, or *physical volume*, is a contiguous allocation of blocks for a specific purpose, such as the organization of a file system.

Partitions are the basic method for coarse-grained storage management; they allow a single physical device to be dedicated to multiple purposes, such as hosting different filesystems, or separating OS installation from user files. If subdivision is not needed, the entire device can be trivially allocated to a single partition.

> A **logical volume** is a collection of physical volumes presented and managed as a single unit.

Logical volumes allow storage capacity from different devices to be pooled transparently (to the filesystem) to simplify the utilization of available capacity. They also enable automated block-level replication in the form of RAIDs [35] for enhanced performance and durability.

MBR (DOS) Partitions.

In the PC (x86) world, support for partitioning was first introduced in 1983 as part of the PC DOS 2.0 release. The boot sector, known as the *master boot record* (MBR), contains a table with four 16-byte entries, defining the boundaries of the primary partitions. The format is shown in Table 4.1.

Table 4.1: MBR partition entry format; offset and length in bytes

Offset	Length	Description
00	1	Status: 0x80 = active, 0x00 = inactive
01	3	CHS address of the *first* sector in the partition
04	1	Partition type
05	3	CHS address of the *last* sector in the partition
08	4	LBA address of the *first* sector in the partition
12	4	Number of sectors in the partition
	16	Total length

CHS addresses follow the legacy *cylinder-head-sector* convention supporting a maximum of 8032.5MiB:

63 sectors/track × 255 heads (tracks/cylinder) × 1,024 cylinders × 512 bytes/sector.

This maximum is commonly rounded up and referred to as *the 8GB limit*, and is a clear shortcoming of the scheme. LBA, *logical block addressing*, is a simple linear addressing scheme which yields integer addresses between zero and the number of sectors less one. For compatibility purposes, there is formula mapping CHS to LBA addresses. The *partition type* provides an indication of the type of file system present on the partition, such as 0x06: FAT32, 0x07: NTFS, and 0x83: *Linux*.

Listing 4.2 shows example output from the *mmls* command (from the *Sleuthkit* [22]) when applied to a file image (`target-64M.dd`) of a storage device. The image starts with an MBR containing the partition table, followed by 1MiB of unallocated space. Next are two partitions: the first one is a 40MiB *FAT32* partition (81,920 sectors × 512 bytes), which starts at sector 2,048; the second one is a (Linux) *ext3* partition of 23MiB, which takes up the rest of the device.

In order to mitigate the four-partition limit, one (and only one) of the partitions can be designed as a *primary extended* partition. This allows it to have its own *secondary* partitions; the latter are known as *logical partitions* in (*Microsoft*) *Windows* terminology. A *secondary extended partition* contains a partition table and a secondary file system partition. It encompases the secondary file system partitions and describes where the secondary file system partition is located, and where the next secondary extended partition is located.

Listing 4.3 and Figure 4.4 illustrate the concepts for a 6GiB target with six partitions. The first three are primary partitions, 1GiB each, formatted with three different *Linux* file systems (*ext2/3/4*). The fourth partition is an extended partition containing three secondary partitions containing *Windows* file systems (*FAT16/32* and *NTFS*).

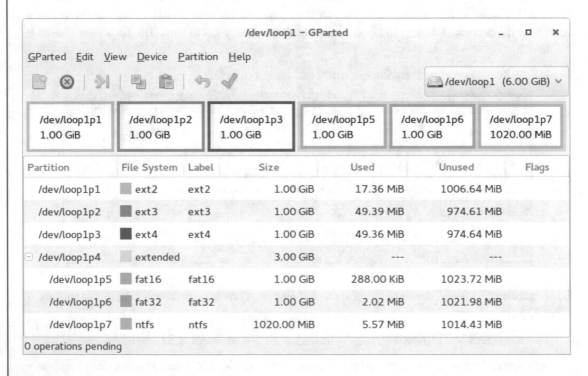

Figure 4.4: Example of a device with six DOS partitions—three primary, and three secondary ones—visualized with the *gparted*.

The reason for this relatively complicated scheme that accomplishes a fairly simple task—describing the split of a storage device into multiple contiguous chunks—is the need for backward compatibility. There is also a fundamental limitation built into MBR partitions—it is a 32-bit

Listing 4.2: Example of a storage device with two partitions

```
# mmls -B target -64 M.dd
DOS Partition Table
Offset Sector : 0
Units are in 512 - byte sectors
     Slot    Start       End         Length      Size  Description
00:  Meta    0000000000  0000000000  0000000001  0512B Primary Table (#0)
01:  -----   0000000000  0000002047  0000002048  1024K Unallocated
02:  00:00   0000002048  0000083967  0000081920  0040M Win95 FAT32 (0x0B)
03:  00:01   0000083968  0000131071  0000047104  0023M Linux (0x83)
```

Listing 4.3: Example of a storage device with *six* partitions

```
     Slot    Start       End         Length      Size  Description
00:  Meta    0000000000  0000000000  0000000001  0512B Primary Table (#0)
01:  -----   0000000000  0000002047  0000002048  1024K Unallocated
02:  00:00   0000002048  0002099199  0002097152  1024M Linux (0x83)
03:  00:01   0002099200  0004196351  0002097152  1024M Linux (0x83)
04:  00:02   0004196352  0006293503  0002097152  1024M Linux (0x83)
05:  Meta    0006293504  0012582911  0006289408  0002G DOS Extended (0x05)
06:  Meta    0006293504  0006293504  0000000001  0512B Extended Table (#1)
07:  -----   0006293504  0006295551  0000002048  1024K Unallocated
08:  01:00   0006295552  0008392703  0002097152  1024M DOS FAT16 (0x06)
09:  Meta    0008392704  0010491903  0002099200  0001G DOS Extended (0x05)
10:  Meta    0008392704  0008392704  0000000001  0512B Extended Table (#2)
11:  -----   0008392704  0008394751  0000002048  1024K Unallocated
12:  02:00   0008394752  0010491903  0002097152  1024M Win95 FAT32 (0x0B)
13:  Meta    0010491904  0012582911  0002091008  1021M DOS Extended (0x05)
14:  Meta    0010491904  0010491904  0000000001  0512B Extended Table (#3)
15:  -----   0010491904  0010493951  0000002048  1024K Unallocated
16:  03:00   0010493952  0012582911  0002088960  1020M NTFS (0x07)
```

addressing scheme, which means that the largest device it can handle is 2TiB (2^{32} sectors $\times$ 2^9 bytes/sector).

GUID Partitions.

To overcome the limitation of the MBR partition tables, a new scheme, the GUID Partition Table (GPT), was introduced as part of the *Unified Extensible Firmware Interface* (UEFI, uefi.org) standard, which replaced the original BIOS [44] interface for x86-compatible hardware. The new specification provides a simple design based on 64-bit LBA addresses and *globally unique identifiers* (GUID). It has three components: protective MBR, GPT, and partitions (Figure 4.5). The first block contains a protective MBR the purpose of which is to convince legacy (not GPT-capable) systems that this is a properly partitioned, fully allocated device. Thus, they will not be tempted to automatically format it without explicit user input.

The GPT exists in two copies: the *primary* one is located at LBA 1, while the *secondary* (replica) at the very last one, LBA -1. The GPT header (Table 4.2) provides basic bootstrapping information and describes the location of the partition entries array. The specification mandates at least 16KiB to be reserved for it, which translates into a minimum of 128 entries of 128 bytes each. Partition descriptions follow a straightforward [beginning LBA, ending LBA] interval format (Table 4.3) and are also replicated just ahead of the secondary GPT at the end of the device.

Filesystem Data Structure Analysis

There are three types of on-disk data structures stored on every filesystem—*internal metadata*, *file content*, and *file metadata*.

Internal metadata consists of the essential data structures necessary to interpret the filesystem from scratch. Carrier refers to it as "file system data" ([23], Ch. 8) but we have opted for a more specific term. The process typically starts by loading the first block of the volume, *superblock* in *Linux* terms, which contains its most essential pieces of information—identifier, version, size, allocation units, location of the root directory, etc.—and traversing other structures, such the map of allocated/free blocks.

The initial creation of the internal metadata structures on a blank volume is known as *formatting*; in essence, it represents the minimal filesystem—one that has a single root directory, and no files. Figure 4.4 illustrates some of the differences among the different implementations: the "used" column shows how much space each of the different systems has allocated initially to its internal metadata. Thus, to organize a 1GiB volume, FAT16 needs 288KiB; FAT32: 2.02MiB; NTFS: 5.57MiB; ext2: 17.36MiB; and ext3/4: 49.36MiB.

The variation is due to different design decisions reflecting a combination of concerns regarding durability and performance. There are also considerable differences in their spatial footprints (Figure 4.6), which has important forensic implications (discussed in Section 4.1.7).

In terms of analysis, there is not much beyond extracting and displaying it to an investigator. Some of the values, such as names and identifiers, may provide important clues about the purpose of the filesystem. Basic consistency checks should also be performed to ensure that there is no *volume slack*, which occurs if the file system does not take up all the available space on the volume. Under normal conditions the slack space would be unusable as no filesystem claims it, but data could still be written to it using the block device interface.

Table 4.2: GPT header format; offset and length in bytes

Offset	Length	Description
0 [0×00]	8	*Signature*: "EFI PART" → <u>45</u> <u>46</u> <u>49</u> <u>20</u> <u>50</u> <u>41</u> <u>52</u> <u>54</u>
8 [0×08]	4	*Revision*: usually <u>00</u> <u>00</u> <u>01</u> <u>00</u>
12 [0×0b]	4	*Header size in LE*: usually 92 → <u>5c</u> <u>00</u> <u>00</u> <u>00</u>
16 [0×10]	4	*CRC32 of header*: computed with this field set to zero
20 [0×14]	4	*Reserved*: must be zero
24 [0×18]	8	*Current LBA*: location of this header copy
32 [0×20]	8	*Backup LBA*: location of the backup header copy
40 [0×28]	8	*First usable LBA* for partitions
48 [0×30]	8	*Last usable LBA* for partitions
56 [0×38]	16	*Disk GUID/UUID*
72 [0×48]	8	*Starting LBA of partition entries array*
80 [0×50]	4	*Number of partition entries*: usually 128 → <u>80</u> <u>00</u> <u>00</u> <u>00</u>
84 [0×54]	4	*Size of a single partition entry*: usually 128 → <u>80</u> <u>00</u> <u>00</u> <u>00</u>
88 [0×58]	4	*CRC32 of partition array*
92 [0×5c]	–	*Reserved*: remainder of block must be padded with zeroes
	|LBA|	Total length = size of block (512/4,096)

Table 4.3: GPT partition entry format; offset and length in bytes

Offset	Length	Description
0 [0×00]	16	Partition type GUID
16 [0×10]	16	Unique partition GUID
32 [0×20]	8	First LBA (LE)
40 [0×28]	8	Last LBA (inclusive)
48 [0×30]	8	Attribute flags (e.g., read-only)
56 [0×38]	72	Partition name (36 UTF-16LE code units)
	128	Total length

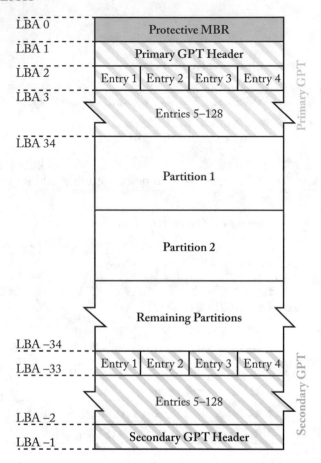

Figure 4.5: GUID partitioning table scheme.

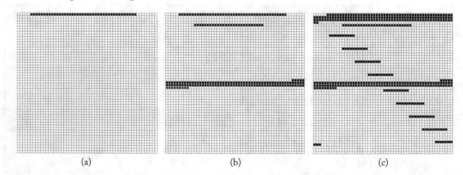

Figure 4.6: Visualization of the *cummulative* effects of formatting (left to right): (a) FAT32 formatted; (b) FAT32 + NTFS formatted; (c) FAT32 + NTFS + ext3 formatted.

File metadata. Conceptually, to create a file, the filesystem needs to: (a) find enough available blocks on the volume, (b) allocate them by updating relevant metadata, and (c) store the content one block at a time. Most of the work is to correctly update the file metadata, which contains *attributes*, such as name, size, owner, permissions, and timestamps, and a *layout map*, which maintains the sequence of clusters in which the content of the file is stored.

As a general rule, modern filesystems cleanly separate the storage of file content from that of file metadata—an allocated cluster may contain either, but not both. (Some filesystems make a performance-enhancing exception for very small files that can fit into a single cluster.) The total amount of metadata is in the order of 1–3% of the total volume space, and is clustered into a few areas on the disk (Figure 4.6). Therefore, all of the metadata can be retrieved quickly and provide the basis for immediate analysis.

Among the most common are *attribute queries* based on name, size, file type, timestamps, etc. Using the file layout information, we can perform *file extraction and content search*. More advanced techniques allow us to reconstruct ostensibly deleted files. Historically, due to performance constraints, it has been impractical to properly delete files on HDDs by overwriting them with zeroes. Instead, the filesystem simply deallocates the clusters freed by a deleted file by marking them as available. Similarly, metadata can also survive, for example, a format operation. This can result in fully recoverable files, but the regular operating system mechanisms provides no means to obtain them.

Consistency checks can reveal parts of the volume that are inaccessible via the normal filesystem API. Inconsistencies can arise during normal operation due to implementation errors or emergency shutdown; however, they can also be constructed deliberately in order to create hidden storage.

Understanding the order in which the filesystem allocates data structures can provide more subtle (if less conclusive) clues on the order in which files were created. For example, a file may be trying to blend in with system installation files by using the same timestamps; however, if its physical location is incosistent with a singular installation event, it can be flagged as an anomaly that can be used to unmask it.

Filesystem journals can be a source of important information about the prior state of the system. The purpose of the journal, *aka write ahead log*, is to enable reliable recovery from faults occuring during critical operations, such as updates to metadata structures. For example, a power failure is always a possibility and can take place at any time. Journaling filesystems write to stable storage their *intended* operations. If the operation is completed successfully, it is marked as such in the log; if it fails, there is a persistent record allowing the operation to be retried, or rolled back.

File content. Direct access to file content blocks allows the examination of data content *in bulk*; for example, a regular expression search can be executed against the entire image and any matched blocks can be mapped back to specific files. Over a large image, this will work faster due to the sequential access pattern, which maximizes I/O throughput, while also examining unallocated

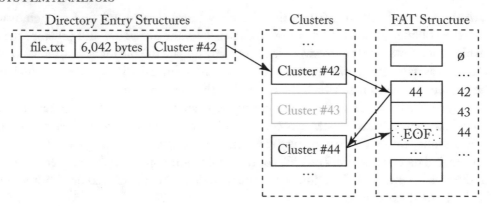

Figure 4.7: Relationships among the directory entry structures, clusters, and the FAT structure. [23]

space. Clearly, the latter can be specifically targeted by using the metadata to identify unallocated clusters.

The examination of *file slack* is another traditional forensic technique; slack refers to the difference between the amount of data in the file and the amount of storage allocated for it. Since storage is allocated in multiples of the cluster size, most of the time, there will be some space left in the last cluster that no other file will use. This is a potential source of hidden storage that, unlike block-level access, requires no special priviliges, and can be utilized via the regular filesystem API.

Other content-only techniques, *file carving* and *fragment classification*, are discussed in Sections 4.1.7 and 4.1.8, respectively.

4.1.5 CASE STUDY: FAT32

The *File Allocation Table*, or FAT, is the simplest among the filesystems in widespread use. There are three "classical" versions of the system, referred to as FAT12, FAT16, and FAT32, and they are nearly identical in terms of on-disk data structures and functionality. The main difference, as suggested by the names, is the width of the FAT entries (in bits) which fundamentally limits the number of clusters that can be employed by the system; it effectively imposes an upper limit on both the maximum number of files that can be represented, and the maximum file size.

In FAT, each file/directory is represented by a *directory entry* structure containing the file name, file size, the starting address of the file content, and other metadata. The content itself is stored in one or more clusters; if a file needs more than one cluster (Figure 4.7), the remaining ones are located using the FAT, which contains an entry for each cluster. The second cluster in the chain is located by looking up the content of the entry corresponding to the index of the cluster. In the example, FAT entry 42 contains 44, which is the next cluster in the chain. Since only two clusters of 4KiB are needed to represent 6,042 bytes, the FAT entry at index 44 contains a special EOF entry, indicating that 44 is the last one in the chain.

The physical layout of the filesystem structures is split into three areas: *reserved*, *FAT*, and *data*. The reserved contains the basic parameters of the filesystem, such as sectors per cluster, label and others. Unsurpisingly, the FAT area contains the FAT structure, whereas the data area contains two types of clusters—ones containing arrays of directory entries, and ones containing file content.

Given the simplicity of the FAT data structures, the independent extraction of files is relatively straightforward. The more challenging part is the recovery of deleted content; as with most filesystem implementations, the deletion operation simply marks the corresponding directory entries as available, and adds the chain of allocated clusters to the free list. The actual file content continues to exist on the media until it is overwritten.

4.1.6   CASE STUDY: NTFS

FAT is a simple design but also one that is prone to serious performance and reliability problems. The *New Technology File System* (NTFS) was developed to replace FAT, and remedies its most serious shortcomings. From the outset, it was designed for reliability, security, and support for large storage devices. In particular, there is an effort to achieve scalability that allows the system to be used effectively over a large range of storage capacities. Before we discuss the essential NTFS data structures, we should point out that NTFS is still a proprietary system and there is no official published specification; almost everything known in the public domain is the result of reverse engineering efforts.

The core concept that underpins NTFS's design is that all data (with the exception of boot structures) are allocated to a file. This applies even to the basic filesystem metadata, which is usually separate in other designs. One of the consequences of this file-centric approach is that the physical layout is no longer fixed—files could be allocated anywhere where there is free space. The entire filesystem is considered a data area, and any block can be allocated to a file.

MFT. The *Master File Table* (MFT) is the key data structure that contains the critical information about the location of all files and directories. MFT entries are 1KiB in size and have a simple format—their primary purpose is to store attributes of various kinds, such as file name and timestamps. The entry has a small header, and the rest of it is used to store attributes.

The MFT is also stored as a file, which creates a bootstraping problem: how do we find the MFT itself? The first entry in the table is named MFT, and describes the on-disk location of the MFT, which implies that it needs to be processed first in order to determine the size and layout of the MFT. The starting location of the MFT is given in the boot sector, which is always located in the first sector of the file system.

MFT entry. Each MFT entry is sequentially addressed using a 48-bit value, starting at zero. The maximum MFT address changes as the MFT grows and is determined by dividing the size of MFT by the size of each entry. The entry also has a 16-bit sequence number that is incremented when the entry is allocated; e.g., if an entry has been allocated five times (and deallocated four times), the sequence number will be five. The combination of the sequence and entry numbers form a 64-bit file reference address (with sequence as the high-order bits).

System metadata. The first 16 MFT entries are reserved for filesystem metadata files. Every metadata file is listed in the root directory, although they are marked as hidden and, by default, are not visible to regular users. By convention, the name of each metadata file begins with a dollar sign and the first letter is capitalized; Table 4.4 provides a list of these system files.

Table 4.4: The standard NTFS file system metadata files [23]

Entry	File	Description
0	$MFT	Entry for the MFT itself
1	$MFTMirr	A backup of the first entries in the MFT
2	$LogFile	The journal used to records metadata transactions
3	$Volume	Volume information: label, identifier, version, etc.
4	$AttrDef	Attribute information: identifier values, name, and sizes
5	.	The root directory of the file system
6	$Bitmap	Allocation status of each cluster in the file system
7	$Boot	The boot sector and boot code for the file system
8	$BadClus	The clusters that have bad sectors
9	$Secure	Security and access control information for the files
10	$Upcase	Uppercase version of every Unicode character
11	$Extend	A directory that contains files for optional extensions

MFT Entry Attributes. As already mentioned, apart from a header, an MFT entry has little internal structure but a list of stored attributes (Figure 4.8). There are many types of attributes, and each has its own format. For example, there are attributes for a file's name and various timestamps (creation, access, modification, deletion). Interestingly, the *content* of the file is also stored as an attribute.

The attribute header identifies the type of attribute, its size, and its name, and has compression and encryption flags. The attribute type is a numerical identifier of the data type; an entry can have multiple attributes of the same type. Some of the attributes can be given a name, which is stored in UTF-16 Unicode in the attribute header. An attribute also has an identifier value assigned to it that is unique to that entry; this identifier is used to distinguish multiple attributes of the same type.

The content of the attribute can have any format and any size, which is what enables NTFS to store the content as an attribute. To facilitate this capability, NTFS provides two storage options for the attribute's content—resident and non-resident (Figure 4.8). A resident attribute's content

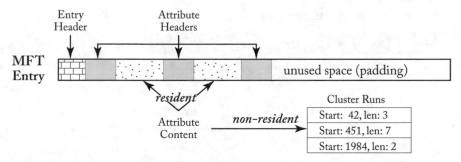

Figure 4.8: MFT entry: resident and non-resident attribute content [23].

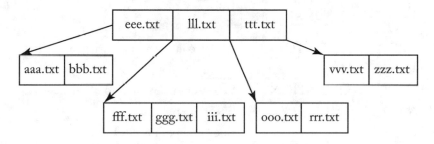

Figure 4.9: Example *B*-tree of file names [23].

immediately follows the attribute header, whereas non-resident ones are stored externally in a series of cluster runs. Each run has two attributes—start and length—and consists of consecutive clusters. For example, the content of a file requiring eight clusters may be stored in three runs: *<start:42, length:3>*, *<start:451, length:7>*, *<start:1984, length:2>* (Figure 4.8).

Files can have up to 65,536 attributes (limited by the 16-bit identifier); NTFS provides the means to employ more than one MFT entry. In cases where additional MFT entries are allocated to a file, the original MFT entry becomes the *base MFT entry*. The non-base entries will have the base entry's address in one of their MFT entry fields. The base MFT entry will have an $ATTRIBUTE_LIST attribute containing a list of all the file's attributes and their respective MFT addresses. Non-base MFT entries do not have the $FILE_NAME and $STANDARD_INFORMATION attributes.

Indexes. NTFS routinely uses index data structures; an index is a collection of attributes that is stored in a sorted order. The most common use is to provide an ordered listing of directory content using the $FILE_NAME attribute. An NTFS index sorts attributes into a *B*-tree; recall that a *B*-tree is a self-balancing tree, which keeps data sorted and allows searches, sequential access, insertions, and deletions in logarithmic time.

Table 4.5: Default MFT entry attribute types [23]

ID	Name	Description
16	$STANDARD_INFORMATION	General information, such as flags; the last accessed, written, and created times; and the owner and security ID
32	$ATTRIBUTE_LIST	Location of other file attributes
48	$FILE_NAME	File name (Unicode) and the last accessed, written, and created times
64	$VOLUME_VERSION	Volume information (only version 1.2)
64	$OBJECT_ID	16-byte unique identifier for the file or directory (versions 3.0+)
80	$SECURITY_DESCRIPTOR	Access control and security properties
96	$VOLUME_NAME	Volume name
112	$VOLUME_INFORMATION	File system version and other flags
128	$DATA	File contents
144	$INDEX_ROOT	Root node of an index tree
160	$INDEX_ALLOCATION	Nodes of an index tree rooted in $INDEX_ROOT attribute
176	$BITMAP	Bitmap for the $MFT and indexes
192	$SYMBOLIC_LINK	Soft link information (ver 1.2 only)
192	$REPARSE_POINT	Reparse point—used as a soft link in ver 3.0+
208	$EA_INFORMATION	For backward compatibility with OS/2
224	$EA	For backward compatibility with OS/2
256	$LOGGED_UTILITY_STREAM	Keys and information about encrypted attributes (ver 3.0+)

4.1.7 DATA RECOVERY AND FILE CONTENT CARVING

One of the early staples of data recovery tools has been *un*delete functionality that can reverse the effects of users deleting data. The most common case is that of users deleting a file and needing to reverse the operation. On a HDD, such reversal is readily achievable immediately following the deletion—the storage taken up by the file's content is merely de-allocated (marked as available) but no actual destruction (sanitization) of the data takes place.

A more extreme example is a HDD that has been in use for some period, and has been subsequently formatted (e.g., by somebody attempting to destroy evidence). The *format* command has the effect of creating a set of data structures corresponding to an empty filesystem. Thus, the normal filesystem interface, after querying those structures, will report that there are no files. However, the reality is that—at that moment—only filesystem metadata has been (partially) overwritten and all data blocks representing file content are still present on the media.

Figure 4.6 illustrates this point by visualizing the blocks affected by reformatting the drive using filesystems of different types. It should be clear that even *multiple* successive formats of the same volume using different filesystems have very low impact on potentially recoverable content. Clearly, as new files are created, the old content may need to be overwritten; however, depending on the file creation/deletion pattern, file content can potentially survive for a long period of time.

Forensic computing, unlike most other types of computations, is most keenly interested in *all* recoverable (partial) artifacts, including—and sometimes especially—de-allocated ones. Unless a user has taken special measures to securely wipe a hard disk, at any given time, the media contains recoverable applications artifacts (files) that are ostensibly deleted. The process of restoring the artifacts is commonly accomplished by *carving*.

> **File (content) carving** is the process of recovering and reconstructing file content directly from block storage without the benefit of filesystem metadata.
>
> More generally, **data (content) carving** is the process of reconstructing logical objects (such as files, database records, and other data structures) directly from a bulk data capture (such as a disk, or RAM image) without the use of metadata describing the location and layout of the artifacts.

File carving is the oldest, and most commonly used, technique and its basic form is based on two simple observations: (a) most file formats have specific beginning and end tags (*aka* header and footer); and (b) file systems heavily favor sequential file layout for better performance.

Put together, these yield a basic recovery algorithm: (1) scan the capture sequentially until a known header is found; for example, *JPEG* images always start with the (hexadecimal) `ff` `d8` `ff` header; (2) scan sequentially until a corresponding footer is found; e.g., `ff` `d9` for *JPEG*; (3) copy the data in between as the recovered artifact. Figure 4.10 illustrates some of the most common cases encountered during file carving:

(a) *No fragmentation* is the typical case, as modern filesystems take extra effort to ensure sequential layout for optimal throughput performance.

(b) *Nested content* is often the result of deletion; in the example, after the initial sequential back-to-back layout of the files, the content ahead and behind file *B* was deleted and replaced by *A*. In some cases, the file format allows nesting; e.g., JPEGs commonly have a thumbnail version of the image, which is also in JPEG. The nested case can be solved by making multiple passes—once *B* is carved out (and its blocks removed from further consideration) the content of *A* becomes contiguous, so a subsequent pass will readily extract it.

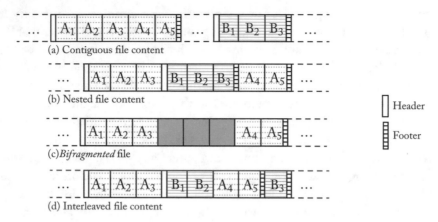

Figure 4.10: Common file content layout encountered during carving.

(c) *Bifragmented files* are split in two contiguous pieces with other content in between, which also determines how difficult the reconstruction is; if the content in the middle is easily distinguished from the content of the file (e.g., pieces of text in the middle of a compressed image) then the problem is relatively easy. Otherwise, the required analysis can be non-trivial.

(d) *Interleaved content* is a more complicated version of nesting and happens when larger files are used to fill gaps created by the deletion of small ones.

This simple approach usually yields a good number of usable artifacts; however, real data is much more complex, which stems from several factors. First, file formats are not designed with carving in mind and rarely have robust internal metadata that tie the constituent pieces together. Some do not even have a designated header and/or footer.

Next, many common file formats have compound structure and combine data objects of various kinds. For example, PDF documents (RFC 3778, [184]) contain streams of compressed text and images, glued together by metadata. Constituent images, such as JPEGs, are stored as-is since they are already compressed. Thus, if a tool identifies an image, it needs to also establish whether it is a standalone one, or part of a compound object. It is notable that even relatively simple formats, like *JPEG*, can contain other objects, like an embedded thumbnail *JPEG*, or an entire XML document as part of the image header's metadata.

Finally, as files are created and deleted, a sequential pass through the raw data will see an interleaving of data blocks from different files, both current and deallocated. This means that the carver (application) will need to use the structure of the data content itself to establish the correct sequence of blocks.

Data carving can be split into two autonomous tasks: *data extraction*—the identification of candidate chunks of content (such as disk blocks, or network packet payload), and *artifact reconstruction*—the reassembly of (part of) the original artifact. Identifying candidate chunks, each of which is a contiguous piece, gave rise to the problem of *file fragment classification*—the classification of the encoding format of a fragment based on its content—which is the subject of Section 4.1.8. Here, we focus on the problem of reassembly.

In the first generation of file carving tools, the extraction phase is based on finding known file tags, as discussed earlier, and the reassembly is based on the assumption that chunk order is preserved on the device. One of the first tools to implement basic file carving was `foremost` [99], which built on prior work at the U.S. Air Force Office of Special Investigations. It uses the basic header/footer approach driven by definitions in a configuration file, and has some built-in parsing functions to handle Microsoft Office (OLE) files [121], which have a complex, filesystem-like internal structure. *Scalpel* [149] is another popular file carver originally conceived as an improved implementation of *foremost*; it utilizes a two-pass strategy to optimize work schedules and reduce the amount of redundant data being carved. Subsequent optimizations [114] allowed the tool to utilize parallel CPU and GPU processing, leading to substantial processing speedups.

The development of new file-carving techniques was pushed forward by the 2006 [24] and 2007 [25] DFRWS Forensics Challenges, which provided interesting scenarios for tool developers to consider. Garfinkel [71] performed a statistical study of actual used hard drives purchased on the secondary market, and found that most fragmented files are split in two pieces and are, therefore, still recoverable with reasonable effort. He also presented a proof-of-concept implementation based on using applications' own parsing routines as a means of format validation.

One of the main problems faced by content carving is the inherent difficulty in disentangling interleaved block sequences belonging to different files. Such situations result in carving tools generating a large number of alternatives, almost all of which are false positives. Thus, it is not uncommon for the amount of data carved out to greatly exceed the size of the source image [151]. Richard et al. [151] proposed a solution to the storage aspect of this problem that, instead of copying the content of the carved files outside the target, overlays a FUSE-based [90] filesystem view of the carving result over the target image. As illustrated in Figure 4.11, this introduces a small overhead of keeping the metadata of this virtual filesystem, but requires no data copying, which saves both space and time.

The authors also demonstrate that the approach can be practically extended to perform (and review the results of) carving on a remote target over the network by using the *Linux network block device* [111]. A similar effort to produce zero-copy carving was developed in parallel by Rob Meijer and resulted in the *CarvFS* [60] system, which also uses FUSE to present a filesystem view of the results.

In [176], Sencar and Memon addressed the problem of JPEG reconstruction. They used the statistical biases of JPEG Huffman encoders to identify fragments encoded with the same code book. Separately, they showed that it is feasible in some cases to reconstruct an image even if the Huffman tables from the file's header are missing by providing a replacement pseudo-header. The resulting image is not identical to the original but is readily recognizable by a human.

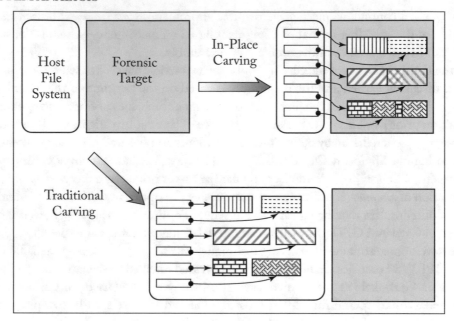

Figure 4.11: Traditional vs. in-place file carving.

Na et al. [125] demonstrate a video recovery method that focuses on the recovery of individual frames. Large de-allocated video files are often partially overwritten and can suffer significant fragmentation. By focusing on frame recovery, the researchers were able to recover 40 to 50% of the data from a corrupted video which was 50% overwritten, and the result was not dependent on the level of fragmentation.

Bin-Carver [86] is a specialized tool for recovering and reconstructing ELF-encoded binary executable files from raw data. The main idea is to use the syntactic rules of the format, as well as the explicit control flow paths present in the binary code, to put together the data blocks in the correct order. The tool has three components: ELF-header scanner, block-node linker, and conflict-node resolver. As the name suggests, the scanner identifies all possible ELF headers using its header tag (magic number). The block-node linker, guided by the structure obtained from the header block and the internal control flow of the code, scans the disk image and tries to identify all the constituent nodes and links them together. The conflict-node resolver removes conflict nodes introduced by the linking phases due to the effects of fragmentation and the presence of non-ELF data to carve out the full executable. The researchers report a recovery rate between 75 and 100 percent for eight synthetic targets developed to simulate difficult cases.

Beverly et al. [13] consider the problem of carving for network structures, such as packets and socket connections, on disk images. This is an unusual take on disk carving as network state is considered transient and the recovery of such artifacts is usually attempted on RAM snapshots.

However, the authors convincingly show that such data persists far longer, usually as part of hibernation files, and were able to extract it. For high-confidence results (that have passed stronger validation tests), network carving yielded precision between 50 and 100% for discovered IP addresses. Tests also revealed the presence of valid MAC addresses that allow for the clustering of images during cross-drive correlation, and for connecting the devices to physical locations via geolocation.

Future Challenges

Looking ahead, file carving is likely to be a useful tool for the foreseeable future as hard disk sizes continue to grow and it becomes ever more performance-critical for file systems to lay out files sequentially. At the same time, the emergence and quick growth in popularity of solid state drives (SSD) presents a new challange. The reason lies in the fact that SSD blocks need to be written twice in order to be reused—the first write resets the state of the block, thereby enabling its reuse. To improve performance, the TRIM and UNMAP commands were added to the ATA and SCSI command sets, respectively. They provide a mechanism for the file system to indicate to the storage device which blocks need to be garbage collected and prepared for reuse.

King and Vidas [101] have established experimentally that file carving would only work in a narrow set of circumstances on modern solid state drives (SSD). Specifically, they show that for a TRIM-aware operating system, such as *Windows 7*, the data recovery rates in their tests were almost universally zero. In contrast, using a pre-TRIM OS—*Windows XP*—allows for near-perfect recovery rates under the same experimental conditions.

4.1.8 FILE FRAGMENT CLASSIFICATION

As already discussed, it is useful to split the data carving problem into extraction and reconstruction phases. The former gives rise to one of the most studied problems in digital forensics—file fragment classification. Informally, a fragment classifier maps every piece of known-contiguous data, such as a disk block, to a particular data type (text, image, video) and container encoding (text, html, jpeg, mp3, pdf). Such classification can be used in various analytical tasks, such as statistical network traffic monitoring, or sampling of a target during triage [74]. Yet, the most compelling use is to aid data carving—once data blocks are classified, it becomes possible to both selectively extract targeted data, and to more efficiently reconstruct the artifacts from their constituent pieces.

Problem Definition

We start with the classical definition of a file as a sequence of bytes stored by a file system under a user-specified name. Historically, operating systems have avoided interpreting the names and contents of files; however, every operating system needs to be able to at least determine if a file is executable. For that purpose, it uses a combination of file naming conventions and a magic number—file-type-specific binary string at the beginning of a file—to perform sanity checking before attempting execution. For example, upon user request *CP/M* and *MS-DOS* will attempt to load any file with a .com extension into memory and execute it; *Windows* marks the beginning of executables with the string *"MZ"* → 4d 5a; *Linux* marks the beginning of executables with the hexadecimal string 7f 45 4c 46, and so on.

For more modern operating systems, it became helpful to associate files with the corresponding applications so that actions like *open*, *new*, and *print* could be initiated by the user from the OS interface. These loose associations between file naming and applications is presented to end-users as a *file type*. It is important to recognize that such types are not strongly connected to the on-disk representation of the artifacts and are not a particularly useful definition from a forensic perspective: the internal data representation of a file type can change (sometimes radically) between application versions. Further, instances of compound file formats can have dramatically different content and, consequently, very different bit stream representations. For example, a *Microsoft Powerpoint* presentation document could be primarily text, or it could include a lot of photos, scanned images, audio/video files, etc. Since the individual components have different encodings, the layout of the data in the file would be very different in each of these cases. To address the problem, we must separate the notions of *data encoding* and *file type* [164]:

> A **data encoding** is a set of rules for mapping pieces of data to a sequences of bits. Such an encoding is ***primitive***, if it is not possible to reduce the rule set and still produce meaningful data encodings.

The same piece of information can be represented in different ways using different encodings. For example, a plain text document could be represented in ASCII for editing, and in compressed form for storage/transmission. Once encoded, the resulting bit stream can serve as the source for further (recursive) encodings; e.g., a base64-encoded [96] JPEG image.

> A **file type** is a set of rules for utilizing (sets of) primitive data encodings to serialize digital artifacts.

Unlike data encodings, file types can have very loose, extensible, and even ambiguous rules, especially for complex formats. As documented in [164], a *Microsoft Word* document may contain a *Powerpoint* presentation, which in turn may contain an *Excel* spreadsheet, which may contain other OLE objects; there is no predefined limit on how deep the embedding can go on. To correctly discover the entire stack of embeddings, one needs the entire file as a frame of reference. Contrast that to the problem of classifying a (small) fragment—it is clear that the fragment may simply not contain enough observable information to make a complete classification. Therefore, we split the problem into three separate questions:

1. What is the primitive data encoding of the fragment?

2. Does the encoding contain recursive encodings?

3. Is the fragment part of a compound file structure?

The second question is strictly optional but is often interesting for simple encodings. For example, identifying a fragment as being *base64*-encoded is trivial but not very informative; discovering that it encodes an image, or text, is substantially more useful.

Any classifier can always make a meaningful effort to answer the first two questions. The ability to answer the third one depends partially on luck as the fragment must contain enough characteristic data from the enclosing container. By splitting the problem into three separate questions, we can begin to build a meaningful and informative evaluation framework. The split also means that establishing the ground truth becomes much more complicated than simply collecting a set of files with a given extension—it is necessary to parse the contents of the reference files to know exactly what is in each evaluation sample.

The *size* of a fragment is a crucial evaluation parameter and performance can vary greatly. At the extremes, if the fragment is too small, there will not be enough data to work with; as the fragment gets too big the results may get noisier as multiple encodings may be detected.

Another aspect of the evaluation process is defining the required level of specificity. For the same piece of data, we can often provide multiple classifications in increasing order of specificity; e.g., text $\rightarrow$ xml $\rightarrow$ mathml. Ideally, classifiers should provide the most specific result.

Statistical and Machine-learning (ML) Approaches

McDaniel and Heydari's work [91] is among the first to consider the (file) fragment classification based on the statistical properties of the data. Their approach is to create for each file a *byte frequency histogram* of the ASCII codes (character unigrams) in the file to be classified. Histograms representing each file type are clustered and compared against the unigram distribution of the fragment. The method was evaluated on a small corpus of 120 files from 30 different file types/extensions, and only whole-file classification was considered.

The observed baseline classification rates were rather modest: 27.5% *true positive rate* (TPR) for the *byte frequency analysis* (BFA) algorithm, and 46% for the *byte frequency cross-correlation* (BFC) algorithm. To improve the results, the authors proposed an alternative approach that created a file type fingerprint based on a correlation of byte positions and the ASCII value at that position. This approach achieved a respectable 96% success rate, but careful analysis shows that it was simply a variation on the traditional header/footer analysis and would not work for classifying arbitrary file fragments (the common case).

The next important piece of work belongs to Li et al. [107] who substantially revamped the unigram distribution approach. The basic idea is to use a centroid, or multiple centroids, derived from the byte frequency distribution as the signature of a file type. One important shortcoming of the published evaluation is that it did not consider fragments sampled from the middle of a file. Instead, the fragments all started at the beginning of the file and the authors considered fragments of 20, 200, 500, 1,000 bytes, as well as the whole file. Counterintuitively, the 20-byte fragments were identified with near perfection, yet the accuracy of the same approach applied to entire files drops significantly (down to 77% for whole *JPEG* files). The authors offer no rationale, but one obvious explanation fitting the data is that the main information signal comes from the header signature, and larger samples dilute it.

Karresand and Shahmehri [98] developed a similar, centroid-based idea and called it the *Oscar* method, which was shortly extended in [97] with the introduction of a *rate of change* (RoC) metric; RoC is defined as the difference of the values of consecutive bytes. Although RoC is used as a generic feature in machine learning techniques, for the purposes of fragment classification, it is primarily useful for *JPEG*-encoded data. It identifies a quirk of the *JPEG* format, which utilizes byte stuffing. The ff code is used as an escape character marking the beginning of all metadata tags; thus, an extra 00 byte is placed after every ff byte in the body of the file. This produces a reliable and highly characteristic ff 00 bigram which has the highest RoC.

The presented results show that, apart from *JPEG*, RoC does nothing to improve the rather modest classification success of other file formats considered. For *Windows* executables, the false positive rate actually exceeded the detection rate for most points shown ([97], Fig. 3); the peak detection rate of 70% is equal to the false positive rate of 70%. For zip files, things look a little better with a false positive rate of 70% when the detection rate reaches 100% ([97], Fig. 3).

Veenman [189] combined the unigram distributions with Shannon entropy and Kolmogorov complexity measures as the basis for his classification approach. He used a 450MB evaluation corpus, employed 11 different file formats, and tested his method on 4KiB fragments. The classification success for most was relatively modest: between 18% for *zip* and 78% for executables. The only standouts were *html* and *JPEG* with 99 and 98 percent detection rates.

Calhoun and Coles [20] expanded upon Veenman's work by employing a set of additional measures (16 total) and combinations of them. The test sets were relatively small—50 fragments per file type—and the authors recognized the need for more subtle testing and performed all-pairs comparison of three compressed formats: *jpeg*, *gif*, and *pdf*; header data was not considered. The results for the different metrics used show true positive rates for the binary classification between 60% and 86%, implying false positives in the 14 to 40% range.

Specialized Approaches

Taking note of the fact that statistical approaches *mistakenly* assume that, in all cases, a file type corresponds to a data encoding with distinct statistical features, Roussev and Garfinkel [162] argue that the best, near-perfect results can only be achieved by hand-building specialized classifiers.

In one of their case studies, they pose the question of how to effectively and efficiently differentiate *zlib*-encoded data (RFC 1950) (in the form a gz files) from *JPEG* data. This is a non-trivial case in that both use Huffman-coding-based compression and have nearly identical statistical profiles. The only differentiating feature is the byte stuffing described earlier in this section. To take advantage of it, the authors pose the classification problem as follows:

Given a fragment of a certain size, what is the probability that a non-*JPEG* fragment will be indistinguishable from a *JPEG* one, considering that most bigrams starting with `ff` are not legal in the body of a *JPEG* image? The criterion was empirically evaluated and showed that, for fragments of size 512, 1,500, and 4,096 bytes, the accuracy of the method is 83.41, 98.50, and 99.97 percent, respectively.

In the same work, the authors built a specialized `mp3` classifier and carver, which used the presense of synchronization markers in the data stream, as well as validation of the frame headers to achieve perfect classification with no false results.

Mayer [44] demonstrated automated construction of long characteristic *n*-grams for the purposes of fragment classification. He introduced the idea of *summarized n-grams* whereby multiple variations of the *n*-grams are reduced to a single pattern. The two principal transformations are the conversion of all ASCII letters to lower case and the replacement of all ASCII digits with the digit "5". The work showed that—for some encodings—long *n*-grams can be an effective solution, especially for whole file classification. Nevertheless, a major limitation is that *fragments* may not contain any characteristic strings.

The Limits of Fragment Classification

Recently, some researchers have started efforts to better understand the limits of classification, especially for compressed data, which represents the most difficult cases.

Penrose et al. [139] study the problem of differentiating between compressed and encrypted fragments. They used nine out of the fifteen tests in the NIST Statistical Test Suite [171] to build a classifier. The essential rationale is that encrypted data fragments (using AES), should be indistinguishable from random data, whereas compressed data using standard methods (such as *deflate*) should exhibit biases.

The researchers used three compression tools (in order of increasing compression ability): *zip*, *bz2*, and *7zip*; and fragments sizes of 4, 8, and 16KiB. The results from the experiments show that: for 16KiB *deflate*-compressed chunks (using *zip*), the method's accuracy can reach 92%; for 16KiB *bz2*-compressed chunks the accuracy tops out at 72%; for *7zip*-compressed chunks the best accuracy is 12%, for 4KiB chunks.

The interpretation of the results is straightforward—as the quality of the compression goes up, and redundancies in the encoding are squeezed out, the output stream becomes indistinguishable from random/encrypted data. Consequently, any classification methods that rely on statistical measures are doomed to failure, and only specialized techniques based on bit-sequence markers too subtle for statistics (perhaps) have a chance of providing reliable results.

In [164], Roussev and Quates demonstrate a technique for distinguishing the encoding of the original, *un*compressed data, based on the characteristics of the observed *deflate* stream encoding. At heart, this is another example of a specialized method, which is able to distinguish among *docx/xlsx*, *png*, and compressed *Windows* executables.

The authors also considered the question of *feasibily*; that is, how big does the fragment need to be in order for it to be classifiable. The results show that for *docx/xlsx* documents, which consist of compressed XML, no compressed blocks exceed 16KiB; however, for compressed *Windows* executables and libraries, the corresponding threshold is 48KiB, with 20% of the blocks having a size above 32KiB. Such results suggest that practical classification of compressed data may *inherently* require larger continuous chunks of data to work reliably, regardless of the method used.

Summary

The problem of file fragment classification is to map a given chunk of data (a fragment) to the data encoding and serialization format of its encapsulating container.

Early work considered a simplified version of the problem by either classifying the whole file, or by sampling from the beginning of the file. Experimental results show that, in such cases, the main information signal comes from the beginning of the file header, making it unsuitable for classifying content sampled from the interior of the file.

Follow-up research considered the classification of arbitrary chunks based on statistical features and standard machine learning techniques. It was successful in distinguishing among broad classes of encoding, such as text, compressed, and encrypted/random; also, some specific features (rate of change) allowed for finer distinctions among compressed formats (*JPEG* vs. *deflate*). However, a critical review of the results shows that there has been no consistent improvement in the classification performance.

Specialized approaches, tailored to each data encoding and format, have been shown effective but have the disadvantage of requiring manual tuning. Further, the designated features may not be present in the fragments being classified. In more general terms, recent research has begun to show that there are fundamental limits on the feasibility of classification in very high entropy data. Other work has suggested that, even for classifiable formats, the *size* of the available fragment may need to be higher than most prior work has assumed; at the very least, classification performance should be evaluated in relation to fragment size.

4.2   MAIN MEMORY FORENSICS

The early view of best forensic practices was to literally pull the plug on a machine that is to be impounded. The rationale was that this removes any possibility to alert processes running on the host and would preempt any attempts to hide information. Over time, however, experience showed that such concerns were largely unfounded and that the substantial and irreversible loss of important forensic information, such as open connections and encryption keys, is simply not justified. Studies have clearly demonstrated that data tends to persist for a long time in volatile memory [36, 178]. There is a wealth of information about the run-time state of the system that can be readily extracted, even from a snapshot.

Process information. It is practical to identify and enumerate all running processes and threads, loaded systems modules; we can obtain a copy of the individual processes' code, stack, heap, code, and data segments. All this is particularly useful in analyzing compromised machines as it allows the identification of suspicious services, abnormal parent/child relationships, and—more generally—to search for known symptoms of compromise, or patterns of attack.

File information. We can identify all open files, shared libraries, shared memory, and anonymously mapped memory. This is particularly useful in identifying correlated user actions and file system activities, potentially demonstrating user intent.

Network connections. We can identify open and recently closed network connections, protocol information, as well as send and receive queues of data not yet sent or delivered, respectively. This information could readily be used to identify related parties and communication patterns among them.

Artifacts and fragments. Just like the filesystem, the memory management system tends to be reactive and leaves a lot of artifact traces behind. This is primarily an effort to avoid any processing that is not absolutely necessary for the functioning of the system. As well, caching of disk and network data can leave traces in memory for a long time.

Memory analysis can be performed either in real-time on a live (running) system, or on a snapshot (memory dump) of the state of the system. In live forensics, a trusted agent (process) designed to allow remote access over a secure channel is pre-installed on the system. The remote operator has full control over the monitored system and can take snapshots of specific processes, or the entire system. Live investigations are an extension of regular security preventive mechanisms, which allow for maximum control and data acquisition; they are primarily used in large enterprise deployments.

The main conceptual problem of working on a live system is that, if it is compromised, the results are not trustworthy. Therefore, forensic analysis is most frequently performed on a snapshot of the target system's RAM, and this will be the main focus of our discussion. It should be evident that analyzing a snapshot is considerably more difficult than working with a live system, which provides access to the state of the running system via a variety of APIs and data structures. In contrast, a raw memory capture offers no such facilities, and forensic tools need the ability to extract semantic information from the ground up. In other words, this is a *semantic gap* problem, and the purpose of memory forensics is to bridge it.

4.2.1   MEMORY ACQUISITION

Obtaining the contents of RAM can be accomplished in a number of ways, depending on the target system. In virtualized environments, the operation is largely trivial—every *virtual machine manager* (VMM) has a built-in snapshot mechanism, which is critical to providing the essential suspend/resume capabilities. In a virtual environment, the opportunity exist to not only examine the snapshot, but also work with the live environment. This is not always feasible, or desirable, especially in incident response scenarios. Considering the problem solved for the virtualized case, we focus on obtaining a (memory) image from a physical system with no virtualization; this is still the typical scenario for client and consumer devices, including mobiles.

If the target system is not currently running, it is possible to use some OS artifacts to obtain the state at the time it was shut down. One high-quality source is the hibernation file, which contains a complete capture of the RAM content so that work can resume from the point of hibernation; laptop computers almost always have a current hibernation file.

The page file, used by the virtual memory system to swap memory pages in and out, can also contain useful information although it is likely to be incomplete; it is often also used to complement a live memory capture by providing the pages that are part of the active workload that have been temporarily swapped out of RAM.

In response to major failures that it cannot recover from, the OS usually creates a crash dump file, which contains the state of RAM as of the point of failure. Although crash dumps are not routinely produced, they can be a very useful starting point in cases of intrusion, as exploit methods may trigger crashes.

Acquiring the content of all of RAM requires administrative priviledges, and our discussion assumes that this prerequisite is met. If this is not the case, then an analyst needs to find a way to obtain those priviledges, which is outside the scope of this book. Generally, this entails some type of attack on the security of the system, such as brute-forcing a password, or exploiting a known priviledge escalation vulnerability. For mobile devices (where the user does not have root access), the latter is applied routinely and often referred to as *jailbreaking*. For Android devices, using the debugging facilities provided for development purposes can also provide a way in [182].

Acquisition Methods and Tools

The physical address space consists of the full range of memory addresses that can meaningfully be interpreted by the memory system. In addition to representing all available RAM, it also maps memory regions for ROM and PCI resources.

The physical address space consists of reserved and available regions configured by the hardware BIOS at boot time. The OS configures hardware DMA (*direct memory access*) buffers within reserved regions for direct access to device memory. The latter means that such regions must be avoided during the acquisition process, as read operations can have side effects and can easily lead to a system crash. In sum, the acquisition tool must address two main challenges [181]: (a) *determine the address space layout*—in particular, identify DMA regions; and (b) *determine the physical memory mapping*—create a page table mapping between regions and the corresponding virtual address space.

OS-mediated acquisition. Most acquisition tools are software based and leverage operating system facilities, which provided access to RAM via the filesystem API via special files.

Unix-family systems have traditionally provided two special device files—/dev/mem and /dev/kmem—to access main memory. The /dev/mem one allows a privileged application to access any physical page *not* located in kernel space by openining the file and seeking to its physical address. The file can also be used to map parts of the physical address space directly into a process's virtual space; this is only possible for addresses that do not correspond to RAM. The /dev/kmem device is different—it represents memory as viewed by the kernel. Namely, a valid offset is a kernel *virtual* address; recall that on *x86* systems, the base address of the kernel's virtual address space is commonly set at 0xc0000000.

The kmem device is potentially very dangerous—it allows *direct kernel object manipulation* (DKOM) by any priviliged process. It gives malware with root access an easy way to conceal its presence [34]. Over time, it became clear that this was, by far, the primary use of the device, which led to its deprecation from the *Linux* kernel around 2005/06. The mem has also been demonstrated as a potential avenue of attack for rootkits [109], but its effects can be limited, and some important pieces of legacy software—like the *X* server—still rely on it. Sylve's work [182] on Android memory acquisition developed ostensibly for mobile devices works equally well on traditional *Linux* deployments.

Windows also features a device object \\.\PhysicalMemory that allowes direct RAM access [19] and is the basis of most RAM acquisition tools. Another option is to employ the MmMapIOSpace() API in order to allow drivers to map regions into the kernel address space. There are also some undocumented system calls, such as MmMapMemoryDumpMdl(), that are typically used as part of the dump handling during a system crash, and can also be employed for acquisition purposes.

It has been shown [181] that the above approaches can be subverted with relative ease. Therefore, Stüttgen and Cohen [181] developed a method that relies on direct page table manipulation and PCI hardware introspection, and does not trust operating system calls and data structures. Such an approach is inherently more resilient and provides the added benefit that enables acquisition from a compromised machine where the analyst operates at the same level of privilege as the attacker (who has the advantage of getting there first).

Hardware-assisted. Carrier and Grand [26] proposed a more reliable hardware-supported acquisition, which relied on outfitting workstations with a specialized hardware module, called *Tribble*. Likely due to additional cost and limited use cases, *Tribble* (and other similar solutions) never entered mainstream IT practice. Becher et al. [10] demonstrated how the *FireWire* interface (IEEE 1394) can be leveraged to access (and potentially acquire) all of physical RAM. It is important to recognize that even hardware-based acquisition could potentially be subverted. Rutkowska [173] demonstrated that a variety of attacks are possible and that basing the solution on additional (PCI) hardware, in and of itself, is not the ultimate solution.

Other approaches. Ruff and Suiche [170] developed a tool that provides another alternative for memory acquisition by converting *Windows* hibernation files to usable memory dumps. Schatz proposed a technique dubbed *BodySnatcher*—which injects a small, forensic OS that subverts the running OS [174].

Forensic Soundness

Although a number of RAM acquisition tools have been in active development and use for at least a decade, there has been relatively little work in attempting to quantify the behavior of such tools. This is not to suggest that authors do not attempt to engineer them such that their impact on the image is minimized, but the overall evaluation approach could be described as "best effort."

The earliest effort to formalize the acquisition method requirements is due to Schatz [174], who put forward three basic criteria—*fidelity*, *reliability*, and *availability*. The fidelity of a memory image is measured by the level atomicity of the acquisition process, as well as the integrity of the host OS footprint and that of the unallocated memory regions. In practical terms, any software-based solution (short of virtualization) cannot achieve perfect atomicity—a capture of the memory state as of a specific point in time—as the reading of memory takes a non-trivial amount of time. On a live system, this means that by the time the process is complete, part of the RAM content would have already changed, and the result would be akin to a "time lapse photograph rather than a point in time snapshot." In some cases, this may introduce inconsistencies that subsequent analytical tools cannot reconcile.

The integrity component of the criterion intends to measure the side effects of the tool itself. Although it does not directly modify RAM content, it must use some resources and may indirectly trigger system actions, such as resource reclamation, that could destroy useful evidence. Therefore, the tool's own footprint and effects on the host system must be well understood and calibrated to minimize its impact.

Reliability requires that the capture method must be robust against all known means of subversion, such as data hiding utilized by intrusion software. Availability refers to the ability to obtain images from all software/hardware platform of interest.

Inoue et al. [93] offer a similar set of metrics—correctness, completeness, speed, and the amount of interference. Correctness is defined as the tool capturing the actual content of the memory locations at the time of acquisition, whereas completeness means that all addressable physical memory is captured. The speed and interference criteria are less formally defined, but the tool should attempt to minimize both processing time and memory footprint.

Vömel and Freiling [191] provide the most rigorous definition of forensic soundness by rooting their approach in the classical work on distributed systems by Lamport [105] and Mattern [115]. Specifically, they use the notions of events and causality to show the connection between *consistent cuts* and the soundness of forensic images. The proposed specific criteria are correctness, atomicity, and integrity. Correctness is defined in a similar fashion to previous work—the tool must obtain the exact content of each memory location at the time of the acquisition; this notion can be applied to both complete and partial memory snapshots.

The definition of atomicity is based on the correspondance between cuts in the space-time diagram of the system (as per Lamport) and snapshots, and a snapshot is defined as atomic if it corresponds to a consistent cut. The intuition behind a consistent cut is based on causility—in a consistent cut (which is a partial history of the system's computation) if an event, such as writing to a memory location, is causally preceded by another event, than if the former is present in the cut, so is the latter. Thus, the corresponding *atomic* snapshot would have internal consistency; for example, if an operation triggers an update to the process list, then the updated version will be part of the snapshot only if the (effect of) the event causing the update is also captured.

The integrity criterion maps the acquired snapshot to a particular point in time. Namely, a region of the snapshot satisfies the integrity requirement with respect to time t, if its content has not been modified after t. Ideally, the entire snapshot should fulfill the requirement, although that may be difficult to accomplish in practice.

4.2.2   MEMORY IMAGE ANALYSIS

Conceptually, the purpose of main memory forensic analysis is to recover as much of the state of the operating system and user process as possible. During normal operation (on a live system) information about the state of the system is available through a wide variety of system and library calls. These routines query, aggregate, and filter the content of relevant data structures to present a readily usable result to the callee. In working with a memory *snapshot*, we immediately lose access to such services.

Therefore, the primary goal of memory forensics is to provide a set of methods and tools to *reliably* extract and interpret in-memory data structures without the benefit of the live code that normally maintains them. A secondary goal is to provide means to access and interpret remnants of processes that were no longer active at the time the memory snapshot was taken. The latter is important because deallocated memory is not typically sanitized (for performance reasons) until it is reallocated.

strings and grep. The simplest and most limited approach to examine a memory snapshot in an automated manner is to use general purpose search and filtering techniques, such as those afforded by the venerable *Unix* command utilities *strings* and *grep*. In particular, the combination of the two allows the extraction of all strings of printable ASCII characters, followed by regular expression filtering. Despite its utter simplicity, this method can provide valuable clues to the investigator as ASCII/UTF text is quite common. It also has numerous limitations, such as the lack of context for any results, which would necesitate follow up manual examination. Also, no binary data objects, like images and internal data structures, can be directly detected, which makes this a technique of last resort.

Content carving. It is entirely feasible to take the carving tools developed in the context of filesystem data recovery (Section 4.1.7) and to directly apply them to any RAM snapshot. The effectiveness of carving will vary depending on how scattered (non-contiguous) the data objects are. The main limitations here are that, again, we have no context for the results, and only data in known file formats would be recovered (no in-memory data structures).

Virtual memory analysis. The first step in providing critical context information for *any* results is to reconstruct the mapping between the virtual address spaces of processes and their corresponding

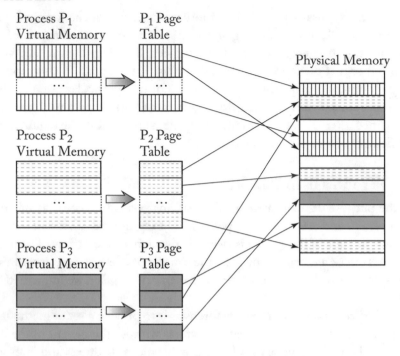

Figure 4.12: Virtual-to-physical memory mapping with page tables.

layout in physical memory. The address space of each process is split into fixed size *pages* (typically, 4KiB) and they all start from logical address zero. Physical memory is also split into *frames* of the same size as pages, and the OS memory manager maps pages to available frames (Figure 4.12). The mapping is recorded in a *page table* and is used by the hardware to perform on-the-fly translation of virtual to physical addresses.

For the *Intel x86* architecture [49], the base address of the (multi-level) page table is stored in the CR3 register of the processor and is reloaded from the *processes control block* structure at every context switch. Once the page tables for all processes are identified and interpreted, it becomes possible to reconstruct the content of the address spaces for each process and to make further interpretation of data structures.

Data structure extraction. From the preceeding discussion, it becomes clear that the identification of the linked list of process control blocks is a critical first step in mapping out the address space. There are two complimentary approaches to identifying in-memory data structures—carving and profiling. Carving involves a sequential scan of (part of) memory in search of a specific signature—string or regular expression—that is present in the content of the structure. For example, *Windows XP* process structures always begin with the hexadecimal values 03 00 1b 00, so a complete scan should identify all process structures. However, it is critical to use additional consistency checks and invariants to filter out false positives, and to identify which structures are live and which ones are remnants of prior executions.

The problem with regular expression signatures is that they do not always exist and they could be modified by malware in order to evade forensic analysis. As demonstrated by Dolan-Gavitt et al. [56] many of the fields in the process structure are not essential to the normal function of the system and can be manipulated. Therefore, the authors identified more complex constraints that involve only critical fields. More generally, important structures like the process control block appear as part of multiple more complex structures; it is not feasible for a process to be absent from *all* kernel structures and to still be active. As an illustration, consider the (partial) output of the *Volatility* [65] `psxview` plugin shown below. It performs process search using several different methods and a normal process would show up in all cases, whereas the hidden one will be absent from one or more of the enumerations.

```
$ python vol.py -f prolaco.vmem psxview
Volatility Foundation Volatility Framework 2.4
Offset(P)  Name             PID  pslist psscan thrdproc pspcid csrss session deskthrd
---------- ---------------- ---- ------ ------ -------- ------ ----- ------- --------
0x05f47020 lsass.exe         688 True   True   True     True   True  True    True
0x0113f648 1_doc_RCData_61  1336 False  True   True     True   True  True    True
0x04a065d0 explorer.exe     1724 True   True   True     True   True  True    True
0x066f0978 winlogon.exe      632 True   True   True     True   True  True    True
0x01122910 svchost.exe      1028 True   True   True     True   True  True    True
0x04bc97c8 VMwareTray.exe    432 True   True   True     True   True  True    True
0x0211ab28 TPAutoConnSvc.e  1968 True   True   True     True   True  True    True
0x05471020 smss.exe          544 True   True   True     True   False False   False
0x066f0da0 csrss.exe         608 True   True   True     True   False True    True
0x01214660 System              4 True   True   True     True   False False   False
0x0640ac10 msiexec.exe      1144 False  True   False    False  False False   False
0x005f23a0 rundll32.exe     1260 False  True   False    False  False False   False
[snip]
```

Scanning is complemented by memory profiles, which contain the layout of core kernel data structures for a specific kernel version. Generating a correct profile is a challenging task, although the issues are different depending on the target. For closed systems, like *Windows*, the main problem is that there is no documentation, so everything needs to be reverse-engineered. Most knowledge is the result of painstaking manual efforts, and systems like *Volatility* are released with a number of built-in profiles. Cohen [43] showed that the speed and reliability of the reverse-engineering process can be dramatically improved. By following the automated procedures, the *Rekall* [42] team was able to generate a repository of hundreds of profiles that can be obtained on demand.

Process analysis. The most common process analysis involves the above described consistency checking of kernel structures to identify hidden processes and the extraction of the process' address space. The latter is the starting point for all application-level memory analysis and can provide the right context for a variety of scanning techniques. There has been relative little research with respect to application memory analysis. One of the more prominent examples is the work by Case and Richard [31], which investigated the operation of the *Objective C* runtime and developed algorithms to detect advanced malware attacks.

Registry analysis. The *Windows* registry is a central, hierarchical, key-value repository for configuration options of the operating system and user applications. Most keys are grouped into several *hives*, which are persistently stored, and the examination of on-disk registry files is considered a solved problem. However, a number of volatile hives, such as HKLM_HARDWARE, exist only in RAM and are recreated every time the system is booted.

As it turns out, obtaining keys and values from an image is a more involved process, as space for the hives is allocated from the paged pool, which can result in non-contiguous allocations. Therefore, it is necessary to traverse a *cell index* structure in order to obtain the correct mapping between a cell and its virtual address. As a result, it is possible to extract the list of open keys and their corresponding values [55].

File analysis. Inspecting the list of open files and dynamically loaded libraries (DLLs) a program is referencing is one key technique to unmask potential compromises. However, it is possible for an attacker to manipulate the kernel data structures and remain undetected. For instance, an adversary might inject a malicious dynamically linked library in the address space of a legitimate process by exploiting a vulnerability to hide her presence on the target machine.

For *Windows*, Dolan-Gavitt [54] proposed a more reliable technique that is harder to subvert, and uses Virtual Address Descriptors (VADs). VAD is a kernel data structure that is managed by the memory manager to keep track of allocated memory ranges [172]. It stores information about the start and end of the respective addresses as well as additional access and descriptor flags. Each time a process reserves address space, a VAD is created and added to a self-balancing tree. Ultimately, the entire list of loaded modules can be retrieved by traversing the VAD tree from top to bottom. It is also possible to reconstruct the contents of memory-mapped files, including executables.

4.3   NETWORK FORENSICS

Network forensics, according to its original definition by Marcus Ranum—the creator of *Network Flight Recorder* [148]—refers to "the capture, recording, and analysis of network events in order to discover the source of security attacks" [147]. Although security incidents are by far the main reason for conducting network forensic analysis, it is useful to take a broader view of forensics and consider any (partial) reconstruction of the history of network events as an instance of network forensics.

Conceptually, there are two separate sources of information in the network traffic—the *metadata* contained in packet headers, and the actual *data* content (or payload). Headers contain limited, but important, information regarding the connection, such as source and destination hosts and port numbers, connection status, amount of data transferred, etc. Combined with timestamp data captured during the acquisition process, it becomes possible to build statistical profiles of typical traffic patterns and, by extension, to look for anomalies that may be of significance. General purpose intrusion detection/prevention systems (IDS/IPS), such as *Snort* and *Bro*, work primarily with the metadata and seek to make decisions in real time.

In contrast, *network forensics analysis tools* (NFAT) [46, 70] work with whole-packet captures, although the capture itself is usually targeted to manage the resulting volume of data. Capturing full packets allows for in-depth analysis, including the reconstruction of packet flows, and allows for the examination of application-level protocol interactions, as well as the retrieval of any data that may have been sent by users (in the form of attachments, for example).

Although initially a distinct class of tools, NFAT never really developed as a separate category of software products. They became part of the larger category of comprehensive network security tools, which include a number of functions like distributed monitoring, intrusion detection/prevention, deep-packet inspection (of payload content), application proxies, etc.

Much of practical network forensics in legal cases is performed manually using general purpose network capture analysis tools. Among open source tools, these include *Wireshark* (wireshar.org)—originally named *Ethereal*—for interactive exploration, and *tcpdump*, *tcpflow*, *Ngrep*, and *SiLK*, among many [140], for automated processing.

PyFlag.   PyFlag [39, 40] is the most prominent tool to specifically target forensic uses—it provides an integrated platform to analyze data acquired from disk, memory, and network evidence sources. The tool provides a small number of basic abstractions upon which the entire system is based.

IO sources. An IO source abstracts the details of the (forensic) image format and presents the tool with a unified view of the different images. The most common formats for storage images are *raw* (as produced by the *dd*) tool, and EWF [119, 152]. The abstraction layer allows the efficient storage and processing of large network captures in PCAP format.

The virtual file system (VFS) is a tree-based data structure, which is the basis for representing all data objects within PyFlag. The VFS is modeled after the structure of real filesystems, and the constituent VFS objects are called inodes. Inodes are strings describing how the object can be extracted from the image, and have corresponding path and filename; the paths determine the directory structure within the VFS. In other words, inodes are human-readable addresses that provide investigators with the source of a particular piece of evidence.

The inode itself indicates how the object is to be derived. For example, the inode `Inet|S1/2|o423:40000|m1|Z100:2000` is interpreted as a recipe for reconstructing the object from the image as follows [40]:

1. The IO source is `net`. **2.** Extract streams 1 and 2 and combine them chronologically through the stream reassembler. **3.** Starting at offset 423 (of the resulting stream) extract 40,000 bytes. **4.**

Parse the data as a MIME message (RFC 2822). **5.** At offset 100 of this attachment is the zip file header of length 2,000; extract the file data.

The filesystem loader is an image-format-specific module which populates the VFS with inodes, and each loader places its inodes at particular mount point. This allows many different IO sources and filesystems to be represented within the same name space; it also allows artifacts from different sources to be correlated. For example, the PCAP loader represents TCP streams with VFS inodes, while the memory loader represents process IDs and other memory structures using VFS inodes.

Scanners are modules which operate on VFS inodes and derive additional information about them. Scanners are cued by the type of the node as indicated by magic number. For example, the *zip* scanner works on inodes representing zip archives and creates VFS inodes for each member of the archive. This allows for subsequent processing to be recursively invoked on the new inodes.

Network forensics with PyFlag.   The system employs several functional modules, which implement the typical processing pipeline of individual packet extraction, packet protocol analysis, TCP stream reassembly, and application protocol parsing (e.g., HTTP).

The *stream reassembler* is a critical component that underpins the entire system and must balance the needs for deep analysis and reasonable performance, as well as the handling of a large number of outlier cases, such as out-of-sequence packets, missed packets, and stream termination. In addition to basic reassembly, PyFlag can also produce *combined* streams. This is helpful for network protocol that follow the request-response pattern, with the combined stream containing the entire transcript of the client-server interaction.

Packet handlers process packets that are not part of TCP streams. For example, a DNS handler can record the resolution requests and responses directly from the network data. *Stream dissectors* work on reassembled streams, and use knowledge of application protocols (like HTTP) to further analyze the network evidence by, for example, extracting files that may have been uploaded.

HTML rendering.   One of the benefits of incorporating different data sources in the same system is that they can be combined to produce a more complete and informative forensic picture. One prime example of such synergy is HTML page rendering—the network capture will contain the request for the root HTML document, but may not contain a subsequent request for embedded elements such as images, and other multimedia content because these have been cached on the host. In this case, the browser cache from the disk can be used to supplement the missing embeds and can result in a much more complete reconstruction of the system as seen by the user.

Web applications, such as Gmail, present an altogether different challenge—the data exchanged between the client and server is often not in HTML, but in JSON, XML, or some proprietary data representation. PyFlag treats Gmail as a higher-level protocol (on top of HTTP), and provides a specialized heuristic scanner, which extracts important aspects of the reverse-engineered conversation, such as subject and message content.

4.4   REAL-TIME PROCESSING AND TRIAGE

Over the last decade, the exponential capacity growth for magnetic media—often referred to as *Kryder's Law* [193]—has created a major performance bottleneck for most forensic software. The average amount of data examined per case at the FBI's Regional Computer Forensics Labs (RCFL, rcfl.gov) grew from 83GB in FY2003 to 821GB in 2013; this corresponds to a compound annual growth rate (CAGR) of 26% (Figure 4.13).

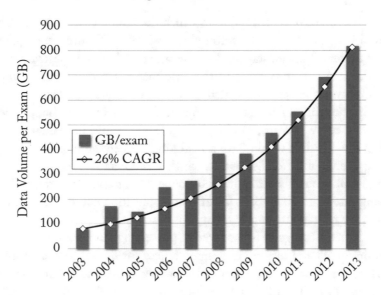

Figure 4.13: Average amount of data per forensic examination based on RCFL Annual Reports FY2003-2013 (https://www.rcfl.gov/downloads).

This growth, coupled with the slow developments in forensic software, has led to an increase in case backlog at forensic labs. For example, a 2016 US DOJ audit of the New Jersey RCFL [187] found that there were 194 service requests that were not closed within 60 days, including 39 that were more than a year old. Every month between January and June of 2015, the fraction of cases open for at least a year varied between 17 and 22%.

An earlier DOJ Audit Report [186] shows that, across the 16 RCFL units, there were 1,566 open requests as of August 2014. Of these, almost 60% were over 90 days outstanding: 381 (24.3%) were between 91 and 180 days old, 290 (18.5%)—between 6 and 12 months, and 262 (16.7%) were over a year old.

Although part of the reason for the backlogs is likely organizational, they do bring into focus the need to make case turnaround time a first-class requirement for forensic tools. In the following section we formalize this by borrowing concepts from real-time computing.

4.4.1   REAL-TIME COMPUTING

Real-time computations are distinguished by the fact that they have explicit deadlines by which they must be completed; otherwise, the computation is considered incorrect. Conceptually, any interactive computation can be viewed as having a deadline (even if not explicitly specified) as users have implied timeliness expectations. In practice, the term "real-time system" (RTS) is used more narrowly to describe a system that has a short deadline (typically on the order of milliseconds) to react to external input.

Systems, such as an airplane autopilot, in which the failure of tasks to meet their deadlines can have catastrophic consequences, are referred to as *hard* RTS, and are engineered such that deadlines are met under all circumstances. On the other end of the spectrum are soft RTS, in which the cost of missing some fraction of the deadlines is tolerable. For example, HD video playback runs at 60 frames per second, which means that every 16.5ms the hardware will automatically render the current content of the frame buffer. This implies that a video player must produce a new frame every 16.5 ms, or else the old frame would be rendered. In practice, occasionally missing the deadline would have a negligible perceptual effect. Video playback is an example of a particular type of RTS—one in which a predictable amount of data needs to be processed per time unit. Thus, the real-time requirement is often specified *implicitly* as the average data processing rate (e.g., 100MB/s). Clearly, an application could miss some of the internal deadlines yet meet the overall rate requirement; this is acceptable.

The soft RTS model is a good fit for forensic processing, and is a suitable means of driving performance requirements and informing design choices for digital forensic tools. The focus of this discussion is on the routine computational tasks performed by the forensic software, such as hashing, indexing, and filtering. There are numerous external factors, such as logistical and judicial restrictions, that directly affect the length of an investigation; these are beyond our scope, but could potentially be modeled and incorporated into the requirements at a later stage.

4.4.2   FORENSIC COMPUTING WITH DEADLINES

Historically, forensics is viewed as an open-ended, post-mortem analysis; the implied assumption is that the process can take as long as needed to accomplish its goals. This is reflected in the canonical procedural model [100], which prescribes a linear processing model consisting of acquisition, examination, analysis, and reporting; a slightly more detailed processing pipeline [88] also incorporates pre- and post-examination steps: preparation and archiving (Figure 4.14). None of the traditional models and definitions mention timeliness as a requirement.

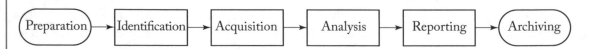

Figure 4.14: Canonical stages of forensic processing.

In the real world, investigations *do* have deadlines. These may vary (depending on the type of case) from hours to months; however, they are relatively inelastic. By way of example, it is not unacceptable for the average investigation to take five times longer because (over the course of several years) the amount of data has grown five-fold. In simple terms, the *case turnaround time must remain stable despite the growth in the volume of data that must be processed.* Based on this requirement, we can derive specific throughput and latency metrics that the system must meet.

The model shown on Figure 4.14 is sequential—each stage's work must be completed before the next one commences. Under this assumption, the only means to improve end-to-end latency is to speed up *all* stages of the process. Unfortunately, long-term technology trends work in the opposite direction. As an illustration, consider the acquisition stage, which is on the critical path for all subsequent processing. Acquisition rates are limited by the maximum sustained throughput from the target drives. For high-capacity HDDs—the main pressure point—acquisition time has increased from 1 hour in 2003 (200GB at 58MB/s) to over 7 hours in 2014/2015: 4TB SATA HDD at 150MB/s [47], or 6TB SAS HDD at 218MB/s [48].

Unfortunately, these best-case estimates (based on hardware specifications) overstate the actual achievable performance, as the software stack imposes its own restrictions. For example, the acquisition rate of the `ewfacquire` tool was benchmarked at 74MB/s using an in-RAM 40GB target, in-RAM output file, on a 2.6GHz AMD processor [165]; thus, the acquisition of a 3TB SATA HDD would actually take more than 11 hours. The additional performance bottleneck here is imposed by the compressed *ewf* (Expert Witness Format) format, and because the tool does not utilize parallel processing. Similarly, the `ewfexport` tool, which reads and decompresses the acquired target, is limited to the rate of 150MB/s (on the same hardware).

The analysis stage routinely incorporates even slower processing, such as indexing and carving, on the critical path. The Sleuthkit Framework (TSK, sleuthkit.org), the de facto reference open source forensic architecture, defines further processing as being organized in the form of pipelines (Figure 4.15).

Although somewhat simplistic (see Section 3) the above sequential model is amenable to the introduction of timing constraints, and parallel processing in the form of pipelining. Specifically, we can define a demonstrably optimal deadline for all computations:

GOAL: *All analytical processing should be completed within the minimum amount of time required to perform the evidence acquisition.*

It is easy to see that the minimum acquisition time, determined by the sustainable throughput rate of the target device, is the exact lower bound on overall processing time—complete analysis implies that, eventually, all data must be read. By requiring that all evidence processing introduce *zero* additional latency, we define a system in which the forensic computation is eliminated as a contributor to case turnaround time. Clearly, this is an idealized solution that is difficult to achieve beyond trivial cases. Nonetheless, it is useful both as a clear aspirational objec-

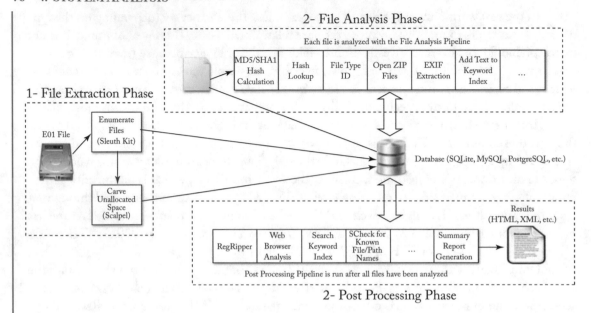

Figure 4.15: Phases of TSK filesystem analysis (`http://www.sleuthkit.org/sleuthkit/framew ork.php`)

tive, and as a benchmark for comparing different solutions. The accomplishment of our optimal goal is dependent on breaking out of the step-by-step sequential model, and employing pipeline parallelism:

- Target acquisition and forensic processing should be performed in parallel at the maximum throughput rate afforded by the target.

  An equivalent formulation is that the processing rate should equal the maximum target acquisition rate. For a modern SATA drive, the reference processing rate is 125–250MB/s for HDD, and 500–550MB/s for SATA SSD. This includes *all* processing that we anticipate for the target.

  To fully utilize available resources, we need a performance-aware acquisition process, which acquires the data in a manner that gives priority to important data and/or data with high processing needs, such as the *latency-optimized target acquisition* (LOTA) proposed in [165].

- Useable partial results should be made available as soon as they are produced.

  This requirement effectively eliminates processing as a bottleneck in the investigative process, and allows analysts to begin productive work almost instantly, and is consistent with the user-perceived notion of real-time performance.

4.4.3 TRIAGE

Over the past decade, the concept of *triage* has entered the digital forensic vocabulary and practice. Although its specific interpretation varies, it generally refers to a quick initial screen of (potential) investigative targets in order to estimate their evidentiary value. Triage is generally perceived as a separate, almost throwaway, effort that—tool-wise—is usually not directly connected to the main forensic investigation. This can be viewed as the result of the performance inadequacies of standard forensic methods, which has forced practitioners to hack together separate triage tools, such as Carvey's Forensic Scanner [28]. Many practitioners in law enforcement refer to this initial investigative step as triage, only if it happens outside the lab and before admitting the media as evidence [137].

To make the distinction clearer, we use the term *triage* to refer to any evidence screening process that is *not* integrated with follow-up forensic analysis. We use *digital forensic triage* (DFT) to refer to initial processing that *is* integrated into the examination process. Thus, we can formalize the latter as an optimization problem:

> **Digital forensic triage** is a partial forensic examination conducted under (potentially significant) time and resource constraints.

In other words, given an available period of time (e.g., 60 min), computational resources (CPU/RAM: 8 cores, 16GB RAM), and I/O resources (120MB/s HDD throughput), there is a finite amount of work that can be performed on the target. The goal of triage is to get to the richest and most relevant information content within these constraints, and present the investigator with the best available information to make decisions. Any case-specific legal restrictions can be modeled as placing yet more restrictions on the optimization task.

DFT is almost indistinguishable from early forensic investigative steps, and it closely follows what experienced analysts do with a target in the beginning. Given more time, such structured triage naturally transitions into deeper forensics.

From a technical perspective, it becomes clear that *latency*—the elapsed time between a query and a response—is the primary performance requirement in triage. Since low latency is also an important design requirement for any forensic tool, there are no inherent trade-offs in optimizing all tools for latency. In other words, we can use the acute needs of DFT as a reason to broadly rethink and improve digital forensic tool design.

Given the low latency (LL) requirement, a triage tool has several choices:

- Employ existing LL methods, such as examining filesystem metadata.

- Develop new LL methods, such as block forensics and approximate matching (Section 5.4).

- Adapt high latency (HL) methods to an LL setup; e.g., by sampling data and/or optimizing the implementation.

- Turn HL into LL by applying parallel processing. In a lab environment, it is becoming quite feasible to utilize tens/hundreds of CPUs; the vast majority of current tools are not ready to take advantage of these resources.

- Use higher-level knowledge, whereby LL methods are combined with the occasional use of higher latency methods. In this setup, a tool could use an inexact LL tool to obtain a hint as to the relative information value of different objects (such as files) that are worth examining with high latency methods.

By exploring in detail these different approaches, we can identify the most promising avenues for research and development. Fundamentally, total latency is the sum of data (access) latency—the time it takes to retrieve the input data—and processing latency—the time it takes to perform the computation.

Latency-optimized Target Acquisition

Based on the preceeding discussion, it is clear that optimizing data extraction on large HDDs needs a more systematic approach to maximize the amount of data extracted from the target. One early effort, discussed in [165], built a prototype system that demonstrates *latency-optimized target acquisition* (LOTA), reconciling the need to read data sequentially from the target with the need to process it in the form of files.

The rationale of the system is two-fold: (a) separate the concern of cloning a target (needed for integrity purposes) from the analytical interpretation of the file data; (b) acquire the filesystem metadata *before* commencing the drive acquisition, thereby enabling the pipelined processing of acquired files.

Filesystem metadata, in addition to maintaining essential file attributes such as name, size, and ownership, also provides a map of the sequence of logical blocks that constitute the file's content. During the preliminary step, all metadata is read in, the filesystem parser analyzes it, and returns a list of file entries; each contains the full-path of the file, its i-node, its parent inode, its mac times, the actual size of the file ondisk, the list of clusters used by the file (in order of usage) and, finally, its resident data (in case the file is small enough to fit within a single entry).

Based on this analysis, the system builds an *inverse* map from block numbers to files and starts reading the target sequentially—as it is normally done—from the first block to the last. The main difference is that the system can use the map to reconstruct (on-the-fly) files, whose contents have been fully acquired, and present them for processing via the regular filesystem API. Disk cloning proceeds in parallel at the maximum sustainable rate.

As illustrated in Figure 4.16, the resulting map is read by the master component and distributed evenly to the pool of agent processes, which may be local or remote. Once the target processing begins, all blocks are routed by the master to the responsible client for on-the-fly file reconstruction. Completed files are written out to the local filesystem, and the registered file handlers are notified; a handler can be any piece of software installed on the system.

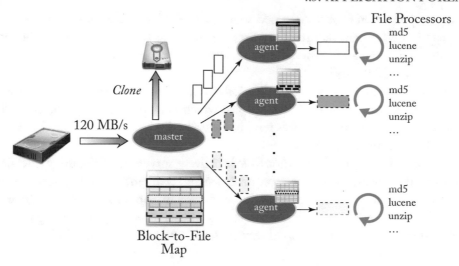

Figure 4.16: Latency-optimized target acquisition: architectural diagram.

There is no hard limit on the number of clients and handlers so the system can be scaled out to the necessary degree to keep up with acquisition rates; alternatively, the system will automatically throttle back to the sustainable throughput rate. Since blocks are sent one at a time, there is no network flooding effect and, since 1Gb Ethernet approximately matches the 120MB/s HDD throughput, the system does not require any special hardware. (With the wider availability of affordable 10Gb Ethernet, a similar system could match the throughput of commodity SSDs.)

The benchmark results confirm the expectation that I/O-bound operations can be performed at line speed. With a single client, file extraction (with no processing) can be performed at 100–110MB/s; with two (and more) it reaches 160–180MB/s and becomes I/O-bound on the tested 300MB/s RAID, which is also used for writing out the assembled files. Unsurprisingly, adding crypto-hashing as a file handler does not affect the observed throughput rate.

Overall, LOTA can increase the average file extraction rate (by volume) 3–4 times: from 25–30MB/s to 100–120MB/s. Over an hour, this means an increase from 100GB of data to 400GB; the relative speedup for smaller files is substantially larger. In a triage situation, there is the need for additional research on how to optimize the read sequence, such that the number of files recovered and processed by the deadline is maximized.

4.5 APPLICATION FORENSICS

Application forensics is the process of establishing a data-centric *theory of operation* for a specific application. The goal of the analysis is to objectively establish the causal dependencies between data inputs and outputs, as a function of user interactions with the application. Depending on whether an application is open or closed source, and the level of accompanying documentation, the analytical effort can vary from reading specifications to reverse-engineering code, data structures, and communication protocols, to performing time-consuming black box differential analysis experiments (Section 3.3.1).

The big advantage of analyzing applications is that we have a better chance of observing and documenting *direct* evidence of user actions, which is of primary importance to the legal process. Also, the relevant forensic traces tend to have a high level of abstraction that mirrors the abstractions of the particular domain.

It is beyond the scope of this work to exhaustively survey the different applications that have been studied; instead, we use the most analyzed and frequently used application—the web browser—as a case study. We also discuss a second class of applications—cloud drives—as an illustration of network-connected client agents; this will serve as a useful starting point for the more forward-looking discussion of cloud services later in the chapter.

4.5.1   WEB BROWSER

Although there are at least four major web browsers in common use, after more than 20 years of development, it is fair to say that their capabilities have converged and—for our purposes—there are hardly any differences of importance. Therefore, we will keep the discussion general, and will refrain from diving into the specifics of the individual platforms; more detailed discussion is available in [134]. There are six main sources of forensically interesting information:

URL/search history. At present, there are no practical barriers to maintaining a complete browsing history (a log of visited URLs) and making it available to users is a major usability feature; most users rarely delete this information. Separately, service providers, like *Google* and *Facebook*, are interested in this information for commercial reasons, and make it easy to share the browsing log across multiple devices. Combined with the content of the local file cache, the history allows an investigator to almost look over the shoulder of the user of interest as they were navigating the web.

Of particular interest are visits to search engines sites. The search query is encoded as part of the URL, and can often provide very clear and targeted clues as to what the user was trying to accomplish.

Form data. Browsers offer the convenience of remembering and autofilling passwords and other form data (like address information). This can be very helpful to an investigator, especially if the user is less security conscious and does not use a master password to encrypt this information.

Temporary files. The local file cache provides its own chronology of web activities, including stored versions of the actual web objects that were downloaded and shown to the user (these may no longer be available online). Although caching has become considerably less effective owing to the increased use of dynamic content, this is tempered by the large increase of available storage capacity, placing few resource constraints on how big the cache can be.

Downloaded files are, by default, never deleted providing another valuable source of acitivity information.

HTML5 local storage is a standard API providing web applications with the means to store information locally; for example, this could be used to support disconnected operations, or to provide a measure of persistence for user input.

Cookies are opaque pieces of data used by servers to keep a variety of pieces of information on the web client in order to support transactions, such as web mail sessions. In practice, most of the cookies are used by websites to track user behavior, and it is well-documented that some providers go to great lengths to make sure that this information is resilient. Some of the cookies are time-limited authentication tokens that can provide access to online accounts (until they expire); others have a parsable structure and may provide additional information.

Most of the local information is stored in *SQLite* databases, which provide a secondary target for data recovery. In particular, ostensibly deleted records may persist until the database is explicitly "vacuumed"; otherwise they remain recoverable at the time of the investigation [95, 195].

4.5.2   CLOUD DRIVES

The concept of a "cloud drive" is closely related to network filesystem shares and is hardly distiguishable from different versions of the *i-drive* (Internet drive) that became popular the late 1990s. The main difference is that of scale—today, there are many more providers and the WAN infrastructure has much higher bandwidth capacity, which makes real-time file synchronization much more practical.

Many providers build their services on top of third-party IaaS offerings, such as *Amazon Web Services* (AWS). Over the last few years, a number of forensic researchers have worked on cloud drives using application analysis on the client side. Without attempting to be exhaustive, the remainder of this section discusses several representative examples of such work. Later in the chapter (Section 4.6.4) we discuss the inherent limitations of client-based methods, and the need for a service-centric approach.

Chung et al. [37] analyzed four cloud storage services (*Amazon S3*, *Google Docs*, *Dropbox*, and *Evernote*) in search of useful traces left by them on client systems. The analyzed services may create different artifacts depending on specific features of the services, and the authors proposed a process model for forensic investigation of cloud storage services. The procedure includes gathering volatile data from a *MacOS* or *Windows* system (if available), and then retrieving data from the Internet history, log files, and directories. On mobile devices they rooted an Android phone to gather data and for the iPhone they used iTunes information like backup files. The objective was to identify traces of the operation of a cloud storage service in the collected data.

Subsequent work by Hale [85] analyzes the *Amazon Cloud Drive* and discusses the digital artifacts left behind after an account has been accessed or manipulated from a computer. There are two possibilities to use the service: one is via the web application accessible using a web browser and the other is a client application provided by Amazon that can be installed on a client system. After analyzing the two methods, Hale found artifacts of the interface on web browser history and cache files. He also found application artifacts in the *Windows* registry, application installation files on default location, and an SQLite database used to keep track of pending upload/download tasks.

Quick et al. [145] analyzed the artifacts left behind after a *Dropbox* account has been accessed, or manipulated. Using hash analysis and keyword searches they determine if the client software provided by *Dropbox* has been used. This involves extracting the account username from browser history (Mozilla Firefox, Google Chrome, and Microsoft Internet Explorer), and the use of the *Dropbox* through several avenues such as directory listings, prefetch files, link files, thumbnails, registry, browser history, and memory captures. In follow-up work, Quick et al. [144] used a similar conceptual approach to analyze the client-side operation and artifacts of *Google Drive* and provide a starting point for investigators.

Martini and Choo [113] investigated the operation of *ownCloud*, which is a self-hosted file synchronization and sharing solution. As such, it occupies a slightly different niche as it is much more likely for the client and server sides to be under the control of the same person/organization. They were able to recover artifacts including sync and file management metadata (logging, database and configuration data), cached files describing the files the user has stored on the client device and uploaded to the cloud environment or vise versa, and browser artifacts.

Outside of forensics, there has been some interest in analyzing the implementation of cloud drive services, such as the work by Drago et al. [57, 58]; however, the main focus has been on performance and networking issues, and—although the results are interesting—their application to forensic practice is very limited.

4.6   CLOUD FORENSICS

Cloud computing is the emerging *primary* model for delivering information technology (IT) services to Internet-connected devices. In this section, we examine both the disruptive implications for current forensic tools, methods, and processes, as well as some qualitatively new forensic opportunities presented by the cloud. The overall expectation is that, after an unsettled period of adjustment, digital forensics will enter a new period marked by substantially higher levels of automation and will employ much more sophisticated data analytics methods.

4.6.1   CLOUD BASICS

Conceptually, cloud-based IT abstracts away the physical compute and communication infrastructure, and allows customers to *rent* as much compute capacity as needed. As per NIST's definition [116], cloud systems have five essential characteristics—*on-demand self service*, *broad network access*, *resource pooling*, *rapid elasticity*, and *measured service*—that distinguish the cloud service model from previous ones.

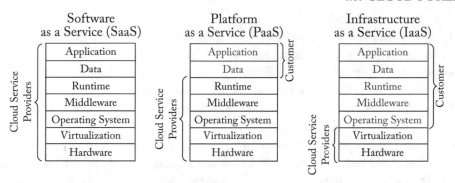

Figure 4.17: Layers of cloud computing environment owned by customer and cloud service provider on three service models: IaaS, PaaS, and SaaS (public cloud).

The cloud, although enabled by a number of technological developments, is primarily a business concept, which changes how organizations and individuals use IT service. Accordingly, it also changes how software is developed, maintained, and delivered to its customers.

Cloud computing services are commonly classified into one of three canonical models—*software as a service* (SaaS), *platform as a service* (PaaS), and *infrastructure as a service* (IaaS)—and we use this split as a starting point for our discussion. In actual deployments, the distinctions can be blurred, and many cloud deployments (and potential investigative targets) incorporate elements of all of these.

The differences among the models are best understood when we consider the VM computing environments as a stack of layers: *hardware*, such as storage, and networking; *virtualization*, consisting of a hypervisor allowing to install virtual machines; *operating system*, installed on each virtual machine; *middleware* and runtime environment; and *application* and *data*. Then each of the models splits the responsibility between the client and the *cloud server provider* (CSP) at different levels in the stack (Figure 4.17).

In a private (cloud) deployment, the entire stack is hosted by the owner and the overall forensic picture is very similar to the problem of investigating a non-cloud IT target. Data ownership is clear as is the legal and procedural path to obtain it; indeed, the very use of the term "cloud" is not particularly significant to a forensic inquiry. In a public deployment, the SaaS/-PaaS/IaaS classification becomes important as it indicates the ownership of data and service responsibilities. Figure 4.17 shows the typical ownership of layers by customer and service providers under different service models. In hybrid deployments, layer ownership can be split between the customer and the provider and/or across multiple providers. Further, it can change over time as, for example, the customer may handle the base load on private infrastructure, but burst to the public cloud to handle peak demand, or system failures.

Infrastructure as a Service (IaaS)

In IaaS, the CSP is the party managing the virtual machines, however, this is done in direct response to customer requests. Customers install the operating system, and applications within the machine without any interference from the service providers. Amazon Web Service (AWS), Microsoft Azure, and Google Compute Engine (GCE) are popular examples of IaaS. IaaS provides capabilities to take snapshots of the disk and physical memory of virtual machines, which has significant forensic value for quick acquisition of disk and memory.

VM introspection provided by a hypervisor enables cloud service providers to examine *live* memory and disk data, and perform instant data acquisition and analysis. However, since the functionality is supported at hypervisor level, customers typically cannot take advantage of it.

Platform as a Service (PaaS)

In the PaaS service model, customers develop their applications using software components built into middleware. Google App Engine is an example of PaaS, offering a comprehensive solution for developing, testing, and deploying customer applications. In this case, the cloud infrastructure hosts customer-developed applications and provides high-level services that simplify the development process. PaaS provides full control to customers of the application layer, including interaction of applications with dependencies (such as databases, storage, etc.), and allows customers to perform extensive logging for forensics and security purposes.

Software as a Service (SaaS)

In this model, CSPs own all the layers including the application layer that runs the software offered as a service to customers. In other words, the customer has only indirect and incomplete control (if any) over the underlying operating infrastructure and application (in the form of policies). However, since the provider manages the infrastructure (including the application), the maintenance effort on the customer side is substantially reduced. Google Gmail/Docs, Microsoft Office 365, and Salesforce are common examples of SaaS, which are accessed via the web browser without downloading and installing any software.

4.6.2   THE CLOUD FORENSICS LANDSCAPE

The term *cloud forensics* first emerged in 2011 from the works of Ruan et al. [169], and Dykstra and Sherman [61], who put in the early efforts to define the terminology and problem space. The former used an abstract, top-down approach, which sought to define the area based on general observations about the technology. The latter used a couple of hypothetical cases to highlight the new issues involved in handling the investigation.

Ruan et al. [168] further pushed the examination of definition and problems by surveying 257 members of the digital forensics community about their understanding of the issues. The results are consistent with a transitional period during which professionals have limited first-hand experience. The most consequential result is an overall agreement on the definition of cloud forensics, which was later refined by the NIST Working Group on Cloud Forensics in their report [133]. It focused on characterizing the challenges faced by cloud forensics by (a) identifying the roles of cloud forensics stakeholders, (b) relating each challenge to the five essential characteristics of cloud computing as per NIST's model [116], and (c) categorizing the challenges into nine different groups.

In all, the report spells out 65 separate challenges. A large fraction of the problems are related to data access, ownership, and provenance; specifically, they stem from the aspiration to precisely replicate existing methods in a different environment. For example, a number of issues stem from the assumption that the logical evidence is extracted from (the reconstruction of) physical media. This implies access to storage media and the low-level infrastructure of the provider, which creates significant technical, procedural, and legal issues.

The problem with this approach is that ownership of the infrastructure is no longer in the hands of clients (Figure 4.17) and, in the case of the public cloud, the infrastructure is shared at a fine granularity in both space and time. As a result, physical acquisition becomes unreasonably intrusive and, therefore, not readily available. In other words, the insistence on replicating traditional forensic practices, while understandable, creates significant costs and disinsentives for the providers. Over time, as forensic examiners become more familiar with cloud environments, forensic practice is likely to adopt an updated model that works *with* the providers' infrastructure.

Another important class of concerns revolves around the lack of standardization across cloud data sources and formats. This is due, in large part, to the fact that cloud IT practices are still evolving and maturing at a rapid pace. Cloud customers are learning what they need from providers, and a lot of their needs are focused on having a comprehensive accounting of all aspects of the service's behavior. Further, they have a vested economic interest in pushing for standardized protocols for accessing such information in order to avoid provider lock-in. This trend will take some time to play out, but—in the medium term—is likely to alleviate a lot of today's standardization concerns.

Our discussion follows the premise put forward in [161, 163] and [159] that cloud IT represents, from the point of view of forensics, a disruptive new *technical* challenge. In other words, the starting point is the realization that both the technology, and the way it is employed is changing. This requires a reexamination of prior approaches, and fast adaptation to the new reality; below, we outline some of its main features.

Logical acquisition is the norm.   The existing forensic toolset is almost exclusively built to feast upon the crumbs of prior computations; this is becoming ever more challenging even in traditional (non-cloud) cases. For example, file carving of acquired media [149] only exists because it is highly inefficient for the operating system to sanitize the media. However, for SSD devices, the opposite is true—they need to be prepared before reuse; the result—deleted data gets sanitized and there is practically no data left to carve and reconstruct [101].

Physical acquisition is even less applicable to the cloud, where data moves, resources are shared, and ownership and jurisdictional issues can be complicated. Cloud service APIs are likely to emerge as the new interface through which data acquisition will be performed; later, we will discuss specific instances of such approaches.

The cloud is the authoritative data source.   Another important reason to tap cloud services for relevant information is that they store the primary historical record of the computation and the interactions with users. Most residual information on the client is transient and with unclear provenance.

Logging is pervasive.   Cloud-based software is developed and organized differently. Instead of one monolithic piece of code, the application logic is decomposed into several layers and modules that interact with each other over well-defined service interfaces. Once the software components and their communication are formalized, it becomes easy to organize extensive logging of all aspects of the system. Indeed, it becomes *critical* to have this information just to be able to debug, test, and monitor cloud applications and services.

These developments point to logs (of user and system activities) becoming the primary source of forensic information. The immediate implication is that much more will be explicitly *known*—as opposed to *deduced*—about the historical state of applications and artifacts. This will require a new set of data analytics tools and will transform the way forensic investigations are performed. It will also bring new challenges in terms of long-term case data preservation.

Distributed computations are the norm.   The key attribute of the client/standalone model is that practically all computations take place on the device itself. Applications are monolithic, self-contained pieces of code that have immediate access to user input and consume it instantly with (almost) no trace left behind. Since a big part of forensics is attributing the observed state of the system to user-triggered events, forensic research and development has relentlessly focused on two driving problems—discovering every little piece of log/timestamp information, and extracting every last bit of discarded data left behind by applications, or the operating system.

The cloud model, particularly SaaS, breaks this approach completely—the computation is split between the client and the server, with the latter doing the heavy lifting and the former performing predominantly user interaction functions. Code and data are downloaded on demand and have no persistent place on the client. Suddenly, the vast majority of the established forensic tool chain becomes irrelevant, and points to the clear need for a different approach.

4.6.3   IaaS FORENSICS

Working with IaaS deployments comes closest to working with physical devices—there are identifiable virtualized counterparts to traditional evidence sources—RAM, storage, and networks. In some respects, it can be easier to work with the virtualized versions due to the possible existence of multiple historical snapshots; also, it is possible to obtain consistent snapshots of working systems without disrupting them. Virtual machine introspection provided by the hypervisor layer enables the examination of live memory and disk data, and can be a valuable tool in investigations involving incident response.

However, in other respects, the investigation process is more difficult as data sources are disappering and historical data is wiped clean during the normal operation of the system. For example, unallocated storage space is automatically sanitized, rendering related data recovery efforts (file carving) useless. VM instances tend to have ephemeral existence—they are launched from a template, and all temporary data is erased as soon as the VM is shutdown; only data explicitly stored by the applications survives the restart.

In [62], Dykstra and Sherman presented the first substantive experimental study of how traditional evidence acquisition tools fare in a cloud environment. They focused on several commonly used tools—EnCase and FTK for storage acquisition, and three tools for physical-memory acquisition—HBGary's Fastdump, Mandiant's Memoryze, and FTK Imager. The overall conclusion was that it is possible to apply these familiar tools to Amazon's AWS service. One major caveat is that the throughput of 2.5GB/hour observed during downloads, as well as the associated monetary costs, put substantial restrictions on how much data can practically be acquired. Under the best method, it took the authors 1 hour to acquire a 1.7GB RAM snapshot and 12 hours to obtain a 30GB disk image. In all cases, the acquisition process must trust multiple layers in the deployment stack. They recommend utilizing the provider-supplied interface to the management plane—the AWS Management Console—as the best approach for acquisition. The Console interfaces directly with the provider's underlying filesystem and hypervisor, and is used to provision, start, and stop virtual machines.

Infrastructure Logging

Subsequent work by Dykstra and Sherman [63] targeted the development of a practical solution to the problem of trust identified in [62]. The resulting tool, *FROST*, is designed to *augment* the existing implementation of OpenStack with trusted logging facilities. The main success of the solution is that both from the point of view of users, and from the point of view of providers, FROST looks like another feature of the environment. Although not foolproof—the system still assumes that the IaaS provided layers are trustworthy—the proposed approach is an example of the technical approach aligning the interests of providers and customers, and (by extension) forensic examiners.

Zawoad et al. [197] proposed a different approach to the introduction of secure logs into IaaS: *Secure-Logging-as-a-Service* (SecLaaS), which stores a variety of VM logs and provides access to forensic investigators. Specifically, the service offers *proof of past logs* (PPL), which can verify whether a log belongs to a particular user or not. The starting point is the assumption that the cloud service provider (CSP) can be *partially* trusted; that is, the CSP generates the secure log entries truthfully, but at a later point, a user, investigator, and the CSP may collude to alter them.

This can lead to a variety of attacks, such as: *privacy violation*—a published PPL is used to infer the log content; *log modification*—colluding user, CSP, and investigator may tamper with the logs via removal, modification, or outright fabrication; *repudiation by CSP*—the CSP may deny a published PPL after the fact; *repudiation by user*—a user may claim that the logs contain another cloud user's data.

The proposed scheme, evaluated via an OpenStack implementation, allows the CSP to store the logs while preserving the confidentiality of its users. Auditors can validate the integrity of the logs using the PPL and the log chain.

Secure Provenance in the Cloud

The SecLaaS work (above) can be viewed as providing a solution to a specific instance of the secure provenance problem introduced by Hasan et al. [89]. Following their original formulation, it is defined as follows:

A *provenance record* P for a document A has two components: the ownership entry for a document, and the log/history of the tasks applied on the document by authorized users.

A *provenance chain* for a given document D is comprised of a time-ordered sequence of provenance records $P_1|P_2 \cdots |P_i| \cdots |P_n$ of length $n > 0$, where two adjacent entries P_i and P_{i+1} indicate that user u_{i+1} obtained D from the user u_i.

An *auditor* is a principal who is designated as an integrity verifier of provenance chain(s).

The *secure provenance* problem can be defined as providing assurances of integrity, confidentiality, and availability to the tasks and ownership provenance records of a provenance chain C_D for a given document D such that:

- Unauthorized parties do not have access to information stored in any of the provenance records P_i (*confidentiality*).

- Adversaries cannot forge a provenance record without being detected (*integrity*).

- Authorized auditors can verify the integrity of the ownership sequence of C_D without knowing the individual records P_i (*availability*).

- User u_i is offered the mechanisms to selectively preserve the privacy of the provenance records pertaining to her own actions, e.g., making them available only to a selected subset of auditors (*confidentiality*). To avoid adversaries from masking illicit actions, designated auditors exist that can read any provenance chain.

Taken together, the above requirements guarantee that the provenance chains are tamper-evident, their contents are confidential, and auditors can verify their authenticity without having to know the contents.

Lu et al. [110] developed a concrete secure provenance scheme, which can achieve information confidentiality, anonymous access to the cloud, and conditional provenance tracking. The particular focus is on achieving two main requirements: (a) *unforgeability*—a genuine provenance record in cloud computing that can effectively attest the ownership and process history of data objects stored in a cloud—an adversary cannot forge a valid provenance record; (b) *conditional privacy preservation*—a genuine provenance provides conditional privacy preservation: only a trusted authority has the ability to reveal the real identity recorded in the provenance, while anyone else cannot. The work provides a formal framework complete with definitions and proofs in the standard model.

Summary. In simple terms, IaaS IT deployments are virtualized versions of conventional, bare-metal IT deployments. Therefore, almost all of the techniques discussed in previous sections (e.g., filesystem and memory forensics) are applicable to data collected from IaaS targets.

IaaS-*specific* forensic techniques are still early in their development, and revolve primarily around the collection and examination of logs. In this regard, forensic needs are aligned with the needs of both customers and providers in that accurate and trustworthy logs are the primary means of enforcing accountability. Experimental work [63, 197] shows that practical solutions can be incorporated into production OpenStack systems with reasonable overhead.

4.6.4   SaaS FORENSICS

The traditional delivery model of the software industry has been *software as a product* (SaaP); that is, software is acquired like any physical product and is installed by the owner on a specific machine, where all computations are performed.

As a result, the traditional analytical model of digital forensics has been physical device centric—the investigator works with physical evidence carriers, such as storage media or integrated compute devices (e.g., smartphones). On the client (or standalone) device, it is easy to identify where the computations are performed and where the results/traces are stored. Therefore, research has focused on discovering and acquiring every little piece of log and timestamp information, and extracting every last bit of discarded data that applications and the OS may have left behind.

The alternative software delivery model—*software as a service* (SaaS)—is subscription-based, and did not start becoming practical until the emergence of widespead Internet access some two decades ago. Conceptually, the move from SaaP to SaaS shifts the responsibility for operating the software and its environment from the customer to the provider. Technologically, such a shift was enabled by the growth of the Internet as a universal means of communication, and was facilitated by the emergence of the web browser as a standardized client user interface (UI) platform, and the public cloud infrastructure enabling universal SaaS deployment.

The cloud renders many device-centric methods—especially those focused on low-level physical acquisition and analysis—irrelevent. It also requires the development of new tools that can work in the new deployment environment where code execution is split between the server and the client devices, the primary storage interface is a service API, and the application artifacts are not persistently stored on the device (although local storage may be used as cache).

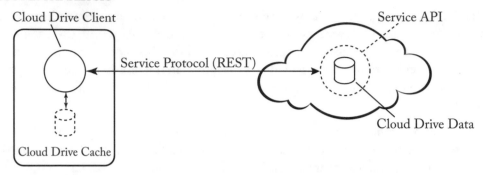

Figure 4.18: Cloud drive service: architectural sketch [161].

Cloud Drive Acquisition Challenges

Earlier in the chapter (Section 4.5.2), we discussed the traditional, client-centric approach to the acquisition and analysis of cloud drive data, which relies on reverse-engineering the functionality of the client agent. Unfortunately, as detailed in [161], such an approach has some inherent shortcomings stemming from the fact that local storage is no longer the authoritative source of the data—it is merely a cached copy of cloud-hosted data (Figure 4.18) with no explicit guarantees with regard to its completeness, or accuracy. There are at least three major concerns in that respect.

Partial replication. The most obvious problem is that there is no guarantee that *any* of the clients attached to an account will have a complete copy of the (cloud) drive's content. As a point of reference, *Google Drive* currently offers up to 30TB of online storage (at $10/TB per month), whereas Amazon offers *unlimited* storage at $60/year. As data accumulates online, it quickly becomes impractical to keep full replicas on all devices; indeed, with current trends, it is likely that *most* users will have *no* device with a complete copy of the data. Furthermore, we need direct access to the cloud drive's metadata to ascertain its contents; without such information, the acquisition is of an unknown quality, subject to potentially stale and omitted data.

Revision acquisition. Most drive services provide some form of revision history; the lookback period varies but this is a standard feature users expect, especially in paid services. It is a new source of valuable forensic information that has few analogs in traditional forensic targets (e.g., Volume Shadow Copy service on Windows) and investigators are not yet used to looking for it. Revisions reside in the cloud and clients rarely have anything but the most recent version in their cache; a client-side acquisition will clearly miss prior revisions, and does not even have the means to identify such omissions.

Cloud-native artifacts. The mass movement to web-based applications means that forensics needs to learn how to deal with a new problem—digital artifacts that have *no* serialized representation in the local filesystem. For example, *Google Docs* documents are stored locally as a link to the document, which can only be edited via a web app. Acquiring an opaque link, without the actual content of the document, has almost no forensic utility. Most services provide the means to export the web app artifact in a standard format, such as PDF; however, this can only be accomplished by requesting directly from the service (manually, or via an API).

In sum, the client-side approach to drive acquisition has major *conceptual* flaws that are beyond remediation; a new approach is needed, one that obtains the data directly from the cloud service.

API-based Acquisition

In broad terms, a cloud drive provides a storage service similar to that of a local filesystem—it enables the creation and organization of user files. Therefore, its public API loosely resembles that of the filesystem API provided by the local operating system. The important point is that an API-based capture process results in *logical* evidence acquisition, not physical, and the latter has long been held as the gold standard of forensic practice.

The problem, however, is that it is completely impractical to apply the exact same procedure used on client devices to SaaS data acquisition. As already discussed, (public) cloud environments pool large volumes of physical resources, and then logically partition them among clients. In other words, there is no single physical device that could be identified, seized, and processed via the traditional tool chain.

As per Figure 4.18, the client component of the cloud drive (which manages the local cache) utilizes the exact same interface to perform its operations. Thus, the service API is the *de facto* lowest available level of abstraction and is, therefore, appropriate for forensic processing. (Hypothetically, lower-level analysis would require the access to the code of the service of the implementation, and the provider's private infrastructure; based on current legal practice, there is no reason to expect that either would be compelled via the courts.) In other words, the software interface afforded by the service API should be treated in the same fashion as hardware interfaces, such as SATA.

Most services provide rich metadata for individual files, including cryptographic hashes of the content, which enables strong integrity guarantees for the acquired data. The service API (and corresponding client SDKs for different languages) are officially supported by the provider and have well-defined semantics and detailed documentation; this allows for a precise and formal approach to forensic tool development and testing. In the following section we discuss, in brief, the basic approach taken in [161].

PoC: kumodd.   Conceptually, acquisition consists of three core phases—content discovery, target selection, and target acquisition (Figure 4.19). During content discovery, the acquisition tool queries the target and obtains a list of artifacts (files) along with their metadata. At a minimum, this corresponds to enumerating all available files; in a more advanced version, the tool can take advantage of search capability provided by the API (e.g., *Google Drive*). During the selection process, the list of targeted artifacts can be filtered down by automated means, or by involving the user. The result is a (potentially prioritized) list of targets that is passed onto the tool to acquire.

Figure 4.19: Cloud data acquisition phases.

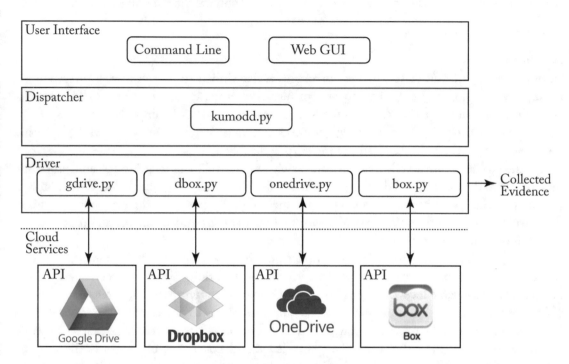

Figure 4.20: *Kumodd* architectural diagram [161].

Traditional tools tend to short-circuit this process by acquiring (by default) *all* available data, and applying data processing *after* the acquisition. However, this approach is not sustainable for cloud targets—the overall amount of data can be enormous, while the available bandwidth could be up to two orders of magnitude lower than for local storage. Therefore, kumodd [161] enables the different phases to be separated, and a more targeted process to be applied, if necessary.

The tool is split into several modules and in three logical layers—dispatcher, drivers, and user interface (Figure 4.20). The dispatcher (kumodd.py) is the central component, which receives parsed user requests, relays them to the appropriate driver, and sends back the result. The drivers—one for each service—implement the provider-specific protocol via the respective web API. User interaction is facilitated via a command-line interface (CLI), as well as a web-based GUI. The general format of the kumodd commands is:

```
kumodd.py -s [service] [action] [fi lter]
```

The [service] parameter specifies the target service, one of gdrive, dropbox, onedrive, and box, corresponding to *Google Drive*, *Dropbox*, *Microsoft OneDrive*, and *Box*, respectively. The [action] argument instructs the tool on what to do with the target drive: -l *list* stored files (as a plain text table); -d *download* files (subject to the [filter] specification); and -csv <file> download the files specified by the file (in CSV format). The -p <path> option can be used to explicitly specify the path to which the files should be downloaded.

The [filter] parameter specifies the subset of files to be listed/downloaded based on file type: all—all files present; doc—all Microsoft Office/Open Office document files (.doc/.docx/.odf); xls—spreadsheet files; ppt—presentations files; text—text/source code; pdf—PDF files. In addition, some general groups of files can also be specified: officedocs—all document, spreadsheet, and presentation files; image—all images; audio—all audio files; and video—all video files.

The important point here is that the service-specific metadata, including crypto hashes, can be used to perform filtering before initiating the acquisition, while the order of the files can be used as a means to prioritize the data capture.

All four of the services use the OAuth2 (http://oauth.net/2/) protocol to authenticate the user and to authorize access to the account. When kumodd is used for the first time to connect to a cloud service, the respective driver initiates the authorization process, which requires the user to authenticate with the appropriate credentials (username/password). The tool provides the user with a URL to be opened in a web browser, where the standard authentication interface for the service will request the relevant username and password. After supplying the correct credentials and authorizing the app, the service returns an access code, which kumodd uses to complete the authentication and authorization process for the account.

Revisions acquisition. The tool automatically enumerates and downloads all the revisions for the files selected for acquisition; the number of available revisions is shown as part of the file listing. During download, the individual revisions' filenames are generated by prepending the revision timestamp to the base filename and can be viewed with the regular file browser, e.g.:

```
(2015-02-05 T08:28:26.032Z)-resume.docx 8.4kB
(2015-02-08 T06:31:58.971Z)-resume.docx 8.8kB
```

Cloud-native artifacts. In the case of *Google Docs*, the local *Google Drive* cache contains only a link to the online location of a document, which creates a problem for forensics. Fortunately, the API offers the option to produce a snapshot of the document/spreadsheet/presentation in several standard formats [82], including text, PDF, and Microsoft Office. To get around the problem, kumodd uses the relevant public API to acquire a PDF version of all *Google Docs* encountered during acquisition. This provides a useable and forensically sound snapshot of the artifact, but results in the loss of editing history of the document (see Section 5.5).

Summary and challenges.   *Kumodd* demonstrates that two of the problems outlined earlier—*partial replication* and *revision acquisition*—can be addressed in full by employing the available public API of the service. That is, all files present on the cloud drive account, along with their prior revisions, can be discovered and acquired without any reference to client state. The API also helps to *partially* address the problem of cloud-native artifacts by obtaining snapshots in standard serialization formats (a more in-depth discussion is given in Section 5.5).

In addition to addressing essential problems of cloud drive acquisition, the work also points to new concerns that require further exploration and research.

Integrity assurance. One of the concerning issues is the fact that not all services provide a cryptographic hash of the content of a file as part of the metadata. Specifically, *Dropbox* only provides a "rev" attribute that is guaranteed to be unique, and is referred to as a "hash" in the API documentation [59]. However, the generating algorithm is unknown and the observed values are way too short to be of cryptographic quality. It would appear that providing a cryptohash for data objects' content would be a reasonable requirement for any cloud API used for forensic purposes.

Pre-acquisition content filtering. Another open question is how to integrate and present the search capabilities built into many of the services, such as *Google Drive*. On the one hand, these could substantially speed up the initial triage of the data; on the other hand, it is unclear to what degree the results can be trusted as we have no precision and recall metrics for them.

Forward deployment. Looking slightly ahead, we will soon need solutions that can be forward deployed on a cloud provider's infrastructure. This will become necessary as cloud data grows much faster than the available bandwidth over the WAN, thereby making full remote acquisitions impractical. *Kumodd*'s web interface is a sketch of this type of solution; the forensic VM instance could be colocated in the same data center as the target, while the investigator controls it remotely. In this scenario, the forensic analysis could begin immediately, while the data acquisition could be done in the background.

Applying Legacy Tools to Cloud Data

Apart from long-term storage and safekeeping, the main reason to acquire a local copy of a cloud target, such as a (cloud) drive account, is the need to apply analytical tools. With few exceptions, our forensic toolset is structured around the processing of files resident on the local file system; that is, they depend on the filesystem API for data access, and cannot operate *directly* on any data stored in the cloud.

Considering the case of cloud drives, it would appear that the solution is to simply create a local copy of the data. The problem, however, is that cloud drives—while broadly similar to conventional file systems—offer a variety of additional metadata not found in filesystems that could be highly relevant to a case. For example, a *Google Drive* file can have in excess of 100 attributes, including both external—name, size, timestamps, and internal ones—image dimensions/resolution, GPS coordinates, camera model, exposure information, etc. Additional properties include user-assigned labels and information about sharing with other users.

Kumofs [159] is a tool that seeks to provide a bridge solution allowing the reuse of file-based forensic tools, while maintaining the ability to query the extended metadata provided by cloud

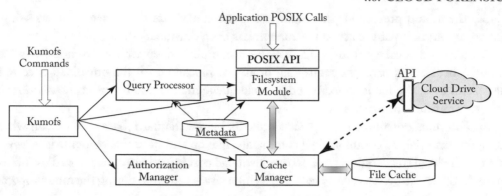

Figure 4.21: *Kumofs* architectural diagram.

services. Specifically, the work provides: (a) a read-only, POSIX-based access to all files on the cloud drive; (b) "time travel" mechanism to examine the revision history of files; (c) filesystem interface for acquiring snapshots of cloud-native artifacts; and (d) a query interface that allows metadata-based filtering of the artifacts.

Design. The starting point of the design is the use of FUSE [90] as the implementation platform; FUSE is a proxy kernel driver which implements the VFS interface and routes all POSIX system calls to a program in user space. This is an established mechanism for providing a POSIX filesystem interface to a variety of data sources. In the context of forensics, FUSE is used by mountewf [117] to provide filesystem access to EWF files; also [151] and [60] have proposed its use to provide an efficient filesystem interface to carving results.

Kumofs consists of five functional components: command line module, filesystem module, authentication module, cache manager, and query processor (Figure 4.21). The command line module provides the interface to all functions via the kumofs command. The filesystem module keeps track of all available metadata and implements all the POSIX calls; it provides multiple views of the artifacts by means of *virtual* files and folders. The authentication module manages the authentication drivers for individual services, and maintains a local cash of the credentials. The cache manager maintains a prioritized queue of download requests, keeps a persistent log of all completed operations, and handles file content requests. The query processor provides the means to list, query, and filter files based on *all* the metadata, and to create virtual folders for the results.

Mounting a cloud drive is performed with the *mount* command:
kumofs mount [service] [account] [mount-dir], where [service] is one of the supported services (gdrive, dbox, box, onedrive), [account] is of the form user@domain, and [mount-dir] is the mount point; e.g., kumofs mount -gdrive joe@example.com joe/

The first mount for a specific account triggers *OAuth2* authentication (as with kumodd). Following the authentication and app authorization, kumofs downloads all the file metadata and concludes the mount process. At this point, the user can navigate the files and folders using the mount point, but none of the actual file content has been downloaded.

Acquiring a local copy of a file can be accomplished either synchronously, or asynchronously. In the first case, the requesting process is blocked until the download is complete; in the second case, the file is added to a download queue maintained by the cache manager, and the process continues its execution.

Synchronous download is triggered implicitly by the standard *fopen* system call, which is invoked, for example, by common shell commands, like cp and cat. File contents is *always* serviced from the local (read-only) cache, so the download cost is paid only once regardless of how it is initiated. The cache persists across sessions; its integrity is validated during the mount operation using the crypto hashes in the metadata.

Asynchronous download is initiated with the get and dl (download) commands: kumofs [get|dl] [files] and standard globbing patterns can be used to specify the target [files]. The only difference between the get and download commands is that the former places the request at the head of the queue, whereas the latter appends it to the end. The qstatus command lists the state of all currently active requests; qlog shows the log of completed requests and their outcome (success/failure).

At any point, the analyst can choose to simply acquire the rest of the files (subject to a configuration file) with: kumofs dd.

Virtual files and folders. Recall that a *Google Drive* account may contain *Google Docs* artifacts that have no local representation, although the API provides the means to export snapshots in different formats. By default, kumofs provides virtual file entries for the different export formats. For example, for a Google document called *summary*, the system will provide four file entries, corresponding to the different available serialization formats:

```
summary.gdoc.docx
summary.gdoc.odt
summary.gdoc.txt
summary.gdoc.pdf
```

It is natural to extend the idea of virtual files to include virtual folders, as it provides the flexibility to handle several scenarios. The first one is *deleted* files; the system provides two views of deleted files—one is through the *DELETED* folder in the root directory and contains the full directory structure of the removed files (in a "recycling bin" fashion). The second one is a per-folder view that, for every folder containing deleted files, creates a *.DELETED* subfolder which enumerates them.

Another case is *versioning*—for every versioned file, such as *summary.txt*, a folder called *summary.txt.REVS* is created, and is populated with file entries corresponding to each available version: *000.summary.txt, 001.summary.txt, ..., NNN.summary.txt* with the appropriate size and timestamps. The version folders provide a convenient means to run processing on successive versions of artifacts. Both the versioning and deleted files features can be dynamically turned on/off, as needed.

Time travel. One aspect of cloud forensics that analysts will have to adjust to is the abundance of time and versioning data. On a traditional filesystem, there is a single instance of the file, and versioning is entirely up to the user (or some piece of middleware). As a consequence, there is no explicit representation of the system in a prior state (e.g., as of a month ago) that can be examined with standard tools, like a file browser.

Kumofs provides the *time travel* (`tt`) command, which sets the state of the mounted cloud drive as of a particular date/time, allowing the analyst to see the actual state of the system as of that time;[2] e.g.: `kumofs tt "Aug-31-2015 5:00p"`. The results can be saved in virtual folders for follow-up processing:

```
kumofs tt "Aug-31-2015 5:00p" state/Aug-31
kumofs tt "Sep-30-2015 5:00p" state/Sep-30
```

Given two (or more) snapshots, an investigator can apply a host of differential analysis techniques. This is directly supported by the *diff* command, which creates a view of the filesystem (in a virtual folder) which contains all files that have been created, modified, or deleted during the period. For example, the following yields all changes recorded during the month of September 2015:

```
kumofs diff "Aug-31-2015 5:00p" "Sep-30-2015 5:00p" diff/Sep
```

Metadata queries. The virtual folder idea is also applied to extended metadata query results via the `mq` command: `kumofs mq '<filter>' show '<keys>'`.

The `<filter>` is a boolean expression on the attribute values, such as `label.starred=="True"`, which would select all files marked with a star by the user. The `show` clause is for interactive display of metadata. For example:

```
kumofs.py mq 'labels.starred=="True"' show 'id,title,labels'
Mounting on /tmp/mq with shadow /tmp/.27oml
1D6o7PsRDIQhgGaTn5jCes50qaeFPZVVbmOgcnsQY9Ts
todo.txt
{
  "restricted": "True",
  "starred": "True",
  "viewed": "True",
  "hidden": "False",
  "trashed": "False"
}
```

---

[2]This is based on the available version history and may not be complete.

As shown in the listing, by default, a temporary mount point is created and all files matching the query are placed there. An extended version of the command allows for a specific folder name to be given by the user.

CHAPTER 5

Artifact Analysis

Once the external (serialized) representation of a digital artifact, such as a text document, or an image, is standardized, it provides a convenient level of abstraction allowing the development of artifact-centric forensic techniques.

5.1　FINDING KNOWN OBJECTS: CRYPTOGRAPHIC HASHING

The lowest common denominator for all digital artifacts is to consider them a sequence of bits/bytes without trying to parse, or assign any semantics to them. Despite this low level of abstraction, there are some very important problems that can be addressed, and the most important one is to identify known content.

Cryptographic hashing is the first tool of choice in investigating any case; it provides the basic means to validate data integrity and to identify known artifacts. Hash-based methods are attractive due to their high throughput and memory efficiency. Recall that a hash function takes an arbitrary string of binary data and produces a number, often referred to as *digest*, in a predefined range. Ideally, given a set of different inputs, the hash function will map them to different outputs. Hash functions are collision-resistant if it is computationally infeasible to find two different inputs for which the output is the same. Cryptographic hash functions, such as MD5, RIPEMD-160, SHA-1, SHA-2, and the current NIST standard SHA-3 [131], are designed to be collision-resistant and to produce large, 128- to 512-bit results.[1]

Since the probability that two different data objects will produce the same digest by chance is astronomically small, we can assume that, if two objects have the same digest, then the objects themselves are identical. The current state-of-the-practice is to apply a crypto hash function either to the entire target (drive, partition, etc.) or to individual files. The former is used to validate the integrity of the forensic target by comparing before-and-after results at important points in the investigation, whereas the latter is used to work with known files. This involves either filtering out common files, such as OS and application installations, or pinpointing known files of interest, such as malware and contraband. The National Institute of Standards and Technology (NIST) maintains the National Software Reference Library (NSRL; http://www.nsrl.nist.gov), which covers the most common operating system installation and application packages. Similarly, commercial vendors of digital forensic tools provide additional hash sets of other known data.

---

[1]A discussion on the known vulnerabilities of cryptographic hash functions is outside the scope of this text.

From a performance and efficiency perspective, hash-based file filtering is very attractive—using a 20-byte SHA-1 hash, the representation of 50 million files takes only 1 GB. Thus, it is feasible to load a reference set of that size in main memory and filter out, on the fly, any known files in the set as we read the data from a forensic target.

5.2 BLOCK-LEVEL ANALYSIS

In addition to whole files, investigators are often interested in discovering known file remnants, such as the ones produced when a file is marked as deleted and subsequently partially overwritten. One routinely used method to address this problem is to increase the granularity of the hashes by splitting the files into fixed-size blocks and store the hash for each individual block. The block size is commonly set to 4 KiB to match the minimum allocation unit used by most operating systems' installations. Given a block-based reference set, a forensic target (RAM capture or disk image) can be treated as a sequence of blocks that can be read sequentially, hashed, and compared to the reference set. In addition to identifying remnants, the block-based approach allows the processing to be performed *sequentially* over the target, thereby utilizing the maximum I/O throughput offered by the storage device.

Garfinkel et al. [74] performed a block-level study, which—among other problems—sought to define and quantify the notion of a *distinct block*. In this context, we say that *a block is distinct, if the probability that its exact content arises by chance more than once is vanishingly small*. If we *know* for certain that a block is distinct, then—in terms of evidentiary value—finding it on a forensic target is almost the same as finding the entire file from which it is derived.

In practice, we cannot have definitive knowledge of the distinctiveness of every possible data block. Therefore, we use an approximating assumption based on empirical data:

> "If a file is known to have been manufactured using some high-entropy process, and if the blocks of that file are shown to be distinct throughout a large and representative corpus, then those blocks can be treated as if they are distinct." [74]

The authors performed a study using a set of 7.76 million files from NSRL [132], comprised of some 651 million 4 KiB blocks. Overall, about 87% of the blocks occured only once; however, out of the remaining non-unique ones, it was observed that they are often repeated within the same file. In other words, the block is not unique but is specific to a particular file. In examining the self-similarity of files, it was established that the fraction of distinct file blocks ranges from 56% for blocks of size 512 bytes, to 88% for 16 KiB blocks.

In terms of applications, apart from the direct use of blocks as trace evidence for the (past or current) presence of known files, block hashes can be used to improve file carving results. The rationale behind the process is that, before running a carving process, all known blocks should be exluded as they will not produce any new data, and may improve the carving process by eliminating fragmentation gaps.

Another example of the utility of block-level analysis is the work on *sdkernel*—a tool for fingerprinting kernel versions [160]. Although the core idea is to apply a byte-stream similarity tool sdhash (Section 5.4.3), the pre-filtering of non-distinct blocks from the kernel images is an essential first step. In particular, an empirical study of 144 *Linux* kernels shows that 26 of the versions have only 7 to 12 distinct blocks. Therefore, in order to produce a sensitive similarity signature, it is critical to extract only the unique blocks and produce the signature based only on them.

5.3   EFFICIENT HASH REPRESENTATION: BLOOM FILTERS

Faced with a large reference hash set, a forensic tool needs an efficient mechanism to store and query it. Of the standard set of data structures, we could use either an ordered list or a hash table. The first choice has the benefit of zero overhead (using an array representation) but incurs an the unacceptable cost of placing a binary search on the critical path of a high-throughput application. Therefore, the hash table is a much more suitable choice; however, one that comes with some extra costs in terms of storage (it is impractical to work with a 100% full table).

One common approach to speed up lookup operations and to reduce space requirements is to use a *Bloom filter*—a space-efficient probabilistic set representation. First introduced by Burton Bloom [14], it is widely used in areas such as network routing, traffic filtering, information retrieval, and database query optimization. Below, we provide a brief description of the concept necessary for our context; a thorough overview of the theory and applications can be found in [18].

A Bloom filter F is a bit vector of size m, with individual elements $F[0], \ldots, F[m-1]$, all initialized to zero. The goal is to represent each element of the set as a unique combination of k bit locations. For that purpose, we employ a set of k independent hash functions, $h_1, \ldots, h_k$, which produce values in the zero to $m-1$ range. To insert an element (a binary string) s, we apply each hash function to it, which yields k values. For each value, $h_1(s), \ldots, h_k(s)$, we set the bit with the corresponding number in F to one: $F[h_1(s)] \leftarrow 1, \ldots, F[h_k(s)] \leftarrow 1$.

To look up an element t, we hash it with the same hash functions and check the corresponding bits; that is, we evaluate the boolean expression $F[h_1(t)] = 1 \land F[h_2(t)] = 1 \land \ldots \land F[h_k(t)] = 1$ and return the result.

It is easy to demonstrate that the filter lookup will never return a false negative result; that is, if the element was inserted, the answer will always be *true*. However, it is possible to have a false positive—a *true* result for an element that has never been inserted but whose bits have been set (by chance) by other element insertions.

The silver lining is that because we can analytically quantify the false positive rates, we can control them by varying the number of hash functions, and the ratio of the size of the filter to the number of inserted elements, in *bits per element*. For most applications, varying the hash functions is not practical—once a reference set is built, it can only be queried with the same hash functions. Figure 5.1 provides an illustration of the non-linear relationship between the number of hash functions k, the *bits per element*, and the *false positive* (FP) rate, for a range of parameters relevant to forensic applications.

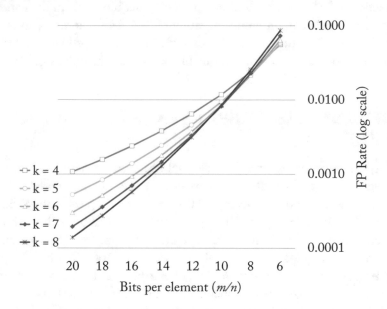

Figure 5.1: Bloom filter FP rates for select hash functions and bit-per-element values.

Due to the large number of hash bits produced by crypto hash functions, it is easy to introduce Bloom filters for the purposes of storing and querying large numbers of hashes. For collision-resistant hash functions, we can treat the individual bits of the output as independent. Therefore, instead of computing k separate hashes, we can take an object's cryptographic hash, split it into several non-overlapping sub-hashes, and use them as if different hash functions had produced them.

For example, we could split a 160-bit SHA-1 hash into five 32-bit hashes, which can be used to build a 512 MiB filter. The same size array can hold approximately 26.8 million hashes; however, if we use a Bloom filter, we could fit 10 times as many elements at the cost of FP rate of 0.13%, which is practical for many purposes. As forensics applications move to 256/512-bit hashes, the effective compression ratios become even greater. If the application requires certainty in the result, a follow-up query can be performed against the original hash to verify it. This is a relatively expensive operation, but it would be applied to a small fraction of the results.

5.4   APPROXIMATE MATCHING

So far, we have considered searches for objects that are an exact copy of a reference object; a much more challenging problem is to find similar objects. In the context of digital forensics, the accepted umbrella term for similarity-based techniques is *approximate matching* (AM). As per NIST's definition, "approximate matching is a generic term describing any technique designed to identify similarities between two digital artifacts" [15].

This broad definition encompasses methods that can work at different levels of abstraction. At the lowest level, artifacts can be treated as bit strings; at the highest levels, similarity techniques could employ, for example, natural language processing and image recognition methods, to provide a level of reasoning that is much closer to that of a human analyst. Considering the whole spectrum of similarity methods, lower-level ones are more generic and computationally affordable, whereas higher levels ones tend to be more specialized and require considerably higher computational resources. Therefore, we would expect an advanced forensic system to utilize a variety of techniques, depending on the goals of the analysis.

For the rest of this section, we introduce the essential terminology as presented in [15], followed by a discussion of essential methods and tools.

Use Cases

It is useful to consider two variations of the similarity detection problem: *resemblance* and *containment* [17]. In a resemblance query, we compare two comparably-sized data objects (peers) and seek to infer how closely related they are. Two common forensic applications include: (a) *object similarity detection*—correlation of artifacts that a human would classify as versions of each other; and (b) *cross correlation*—correlation objects that share components, such as an embedded image.

In the containment case, we compare artifacts that have a large disparity in sizes and seek to establish whether the larger one contains (pieces of) the smaller one. Two common variations are *embedded object detection*—establish whether the smaller object (such as an image) is part of the larger one (PDF document), and *fragment detection*—establish whether the smaller one is a fragment (such as a network packet or disk block) of the bigger one.

The delineation between resemblance and containment is case-specific and the same tool may work in both cases. However, it is important for analysts to put the tool results in the correct context, and to understand the performance envelope of the tools they are using, in order to correctly interpret the results.

Definitions

The notion of similarity is specific to the particular context in which it is used. An approximate matching algorithm works by defining two essential elements—*features* and a *similarity* function.

Features are the atomic components derived from the artifacts through which the artifacts are compared. Comparing two features yields a binary outcome—*zero* or *one*—indicating whether the feature match was successful or not. The set of all features computed by an algorithm for a given artifact constitute a *feature set*. It can be viewed as an approximate representation of the original object for the purposes of matching it with other objects.

The *similarity function* maps a pair of feature sets to a similarity range; it is increasingly monotonic with respect to the number of matching features. That is, all else being equal, a higher number of feature matches yields a higher similarity score.

Classes

It is useful to consider three general classes of approximate matching algorithms.

Bytewise matching considers the objects it compares to a sequence of bytes, and makes no effort to parse or interpret them. Consequently, the features extracted from the artifact are also byte sequences, and such methods can be applied to any data blob. The utility of the result depends heavily on the encoding of the data. If small changes to the content of the artifact result in small changes to the serialized format (e.g., plain text), then the bytewise similarity can be expected to correlate with human perception of similarity. Conversely, if a small change can trigger large changes in the output (e.g., compressed data), then the correlation would be substantially weaker.

Syntactic matching relies on parsing the format of an object, potentially using this knowledge to split it into a logical set of features. For example a *zip* archive, or a PDF document, could easily be split into constituent parts without understanding the underlying semantics. The benefit is that this result in a more accurate solution with more precisely intepretable results; the downside is that it is a more specialized solution, requiring additional information to parse different data formats.

Semantic matching (partially) interprets the data content, in order to derive semantic features for comparison. Examples include perceptual hashes that can detect visually similar images, and methods in information retrieval and natural language processing that can find similarity of the subject and content of text documents.

Researchers have used a variety of terms to name the different approximate matching methods they have developed: *fuzzy hashing* [103] and similarity hashing [155] refer to bytewise approximate matching; *perceptual hashing* [122, 135] and *robust hashing* [69] refer to semantic approximate matching.

Bytewise Approximate Matching

Bytewise approximate matching algorithms are the most frequently used AM algorithms in forensics; they follow the overall pattern of extracting a feature set and generating a similarity digest, followed by a comparison of the digests.

A *similarity digest* (*aka fingerprint* or *signature*) is a (compressed) representation of the feature set of the target artifact. It often employs hashing and other techniques to minimize the footprint of the set and to facilitate fast comparison.

5.4.1 CONTENT-DEFINED DATA CHUNKS

Identifying similarity among text files has a long history and has been in widespread use, especially with respect to code versioning, at least since the introduction of the *diff* utility on Unix. Thus, a lot of early work, as well as related work in areas like information retrieval, has focused on text, although many of the results are usable in a wider context.

One of the seminal works on (bytewise) data fingerprinting dates back to 1981, and was introduced by Michael Rabin in [146]. It is based on random irreducible polynomials, and its original purpose was "to produce a very simple real-time string-matching algorithm and a procedure for securing files against unauthorized changes." Rabin fingerprints, similar to hashing, map arbitrary inputs to a range of integers in a randomized fashion; unlike hashes, the fingerprints have quantifiable collision probabilities and are cheaper to compute than (cryptographic) hashes.

In one of the early examples of the use of Rabin fingerprints for data similarity, Manber [112] created the *sif* tool for Unix. Its goal was to provide an efficient means of quantifying the similarities among text files *at scale*. He used a rolling Rabin polynomial computation to identify *anchor* points in the text that serve as a starting point for a block.

The basic idea, which today is generally referred to as *content-defined chunking* (CDC), has been used in different variations and has been called anchoring, chunking, or shingling. It employs a sliding Rabin fingerprint (or any suitable hash function) over a fixed-size window to split the data into pieces. For every window of size w, we compute the hash h, divide it by a chosen constant c, and compare the remainder to another constant m. If the two are equal (h mod $c \equiv m$), we declare the beginning of a chunk (an anchor), slide the window by one position, and continue the process until we reach the data's end. For convenience, the value of c is typically a power of two ($c = 2^k$), and m can be any randomly chosen number between zero and $c - 1$.

Once the baseline anchoring is determined, there are several ways to select features (substrings). Figure 5.2 illustrates three variations: (a) select the chunks between the anchors as the features (Figure 5.2a); (b) start at the anchor position, and pick the following n bytes (Figure 5.2b); (c) use multiple, nested features (Figure 5.2c).

Without going into detail, we should point out that the numerous variations of the CDC idea have been studied in the context of data deduplication, where the important foundational work is credited to Muthitacharoen et al. [124]. Deduplication is a complex problem as it not only requires the identification of common data, with the purpose of storing it more efficiently, but also addresses the practical concerns of reconstructing the original artifacts.

In contrast, the forensic use of similarity is akin to a search problem, where the reference artifact is presented as a query to the system. As such, it need not have perfect results, but must be able to scale to large data sets.

5.4.2   SSDEEP

The first practical similarity tool developed explicitly for forensic purposes, `ssdeep`, was introduced by Kornblum in 2006 [103]. Based on prior work on spam filtering, it produces a fingerprint by splitting the source file into content-defined chunks, generating a 6-bit hash for each chunk, and concatenating the hashes to produce a (base64-encoded [96]) fuzzy hash. To determine similarity, `ssdeep` treats the two digests as text strings and compares them using an edit

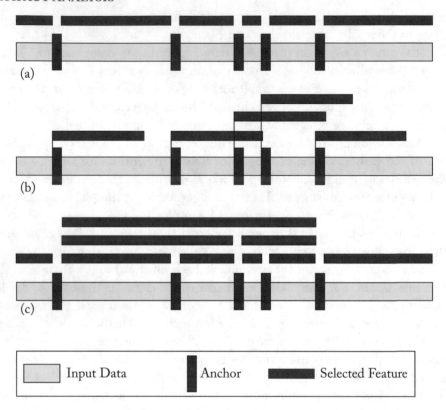

Figure 5.2: Content-defined feature selection: (a) nonoverlapping chunks, (b) fixed size chunks, and (c) nested multi-layer. Different feature selection techniques allow the baseline fingerprinting scheme to be customized for the intended applications.

distance measure, and the result is scaled to a number between 0 and 100, where a higher number indicates higher similarity.

The author made the design choice to limit the signature size to 80 symbols; the main rationale is to present users with a fixed-size drop-in replacement for cryptohashes. To achieve this, the algorithm requires the overall length of the data L to be known in advance. This allows the tool to make an estimate for the value for c that would be expected to produce a signature of the appropriate size.

If the result is longer than the target 80 symbols, it doubles the c parameter and recalculates the hash from scratch until the signature fits within the limit. In practice, a single pass is enough for any high-entropy entropy data, such as compressed or encrypted files; for text data, we can expect an average of 1.3 passes over the input; for Micorosoft OLE [121] documents (doc/xls/ppt)—two passes.

It is clear that the signature is sensitive to file size and places practical limits on the relative file sizes that can be compared; therefore, `ssdeep` produces two fingerprints at two different resolutions corresponding to c and $2c$. This allieviates the problem somewhat but, if the difference in size between the data objects exceeds a factor of four, the two hashes are not comparable. In terms of our problem space, this means that this method can only address resemblance queries, and not containment ones.

There have been several studies on the effectiveness and shortcomings of `ssdeep`. In [157], the performance was examined in several scenarios and one of the main observations was that the the correlation capabilities of `ssdeep` are crucially dependent on a large, continuous block of common data. The minimum size of the common piece must be between 1/4 to 1/3 of the size of the files to guarantee detection (a non-zero result).

5.4.3 SDHASH

The design of `sdhash` takes an approach inspired by the information retrieval concept of *statistically improbable phrases*. The rationale is to pick a set of features to represent an object such that the features are statistically rare in the general population and to compare them with the corresponding features of other objects. The number of features in common can be used as an indication of a degree of correlation/similarity between two artifacts. If *all* the features match, then the two original objects are likely (close to) identical.

The main challenge is to translate this idea from text to binary data and to implement it efficiently. The base `sdhash` feature is a 64-byte sequence (string) and all such features in an object (such as a file) are considered candidates. It is clearly infeasible to either collect, store, or query empirical probabilities for all possible 64-byte features. Instead, for each feature, a normalized Shannon entropy measure H_{norm} is calculated as follows.

First, we estimate the Shannon entropy: $H = -\sum_{i=0}^{255} P(X_i) \log P(X_i)$, where $P(X_i)$ is the empirical probability to encounter ASCII code i. Then $H_{norm} = \lfloor 1000 \times H / \log_2 W \rfloor$. In other words, each feature is mapped to one of 1,000 classes of equivalence.

Using an empirical probability distribution from a representative set, we assign them a *precedence rank* R_{prec}, such that features with the lowest probability have the highest rank.

Next, we define a *popularity rank* R_{pop}, which describes how the R_{prec} of a feature relates to those of its neighbors. To calculate it, for every (sliding) window of W consecutive features, we find the leftmost feature with the lowest precedence rank and increment its R_{pop} by one (evidently, $R_{pop} \leq W$). Intuitively, the rarer the feature, the more likely it is that it will have a higher score than its neighbors.

Finally, we make a sweep across all features and select all the ones for which $R_{pop} \geq t$, where $0 < t \leq W$ is a threshold parameter. During this process, we also perform an additional filtering step which simply ignores all features for which $H_{norm} \leq 100$. This is based on earlier empirical studies [153] showing that features with such low entropy trigger the vast majority of false positives.

Similarity Digest Bloom Filter (sdbf)

Once the features have been selected, each one is hashed using SHA-1, and the result is split into five sub-hashes, and is placed in a Bloom filter with a size of 256 bytes. In the original implementation [155], as soon as a filter reaches 128 elements (features), it is considered full and a new one is created to accommodate further features. Later versions use 160 features as the threshhold [158], which leads to a signature that, on average, requires one 256-byte filter for every 9–10 K of input data, or approximately 2.6%. This process continues until all features are accommodated and the resulting sequence of filters is the similarity digest of the original object. This digest representation is referred to as sdbf, and the tool used to generate and compare the digests as sdhash.

There is a large number of tunable parameters that can provide different trade-offs between granularity, compression, and accuracy. However, it is also important to have a standard set of paramaters so that independently generated digests are compatible. Based on exhaustive testing, $W = 64, t = 16$ were chosen as the standard, although the sdbf format allows for other options as well.

The base operation for comparing digests is the comparison of two constituent filters. Given two arbitrary filters, we can analytically predict their dot product (i.e., how many bits the two have in common due to chance). Beyond that, the probability that the two filters have common elements rises linearly and allows us to define a similarity measure $D(\cdot)$, which yields a number between 0 and 1.

To compare two digests $F = f_1 f_2 \ldots f_n$ and $G = g_1 g_2 \ldots g_m, n \leq m$, we define the *similarity distance $SD(F, G)$* as:

$$SD(F, G) = \frac{1}{N} \sum_{i=1}^{n} \max_{j=1\ldots m} D(f_i, g_j).$$

In other words, for each filter of the shorter digest F we find the best match in G, and we average the maxima to produce the final result. In the special case where F has a single filter, the result would be the best match, which would be the expected behavior. In the case where the two digests have a comparable number of filters, this definition will seek to estimate their highest similarity.

Block-aligned Similarity Digests

Subsequent research [158] showed that a *block-aligned* version of the base digest can be used to increase the efficiency of both the generation and comparison steps. In the original version, the input is examined sequentially, and features meeting the criteria are selected and placed in the digest's current filter. Thus, eventually all the features meeting the criteria become part of the digest.

In contrast, the block-aligned version splits the input into 16 KiB blocks, and generates one constituent 256-byte Bloom filter for every such block. Under this scheme, we expect to find (on average) more than 160 features meeting the minimum criteria; therefore, the algorithm picks the best 192 features (those that maximize the value of the threshold t). It is also possible that the block may contain fewer than 160 features that meet the minimum criteria, or even no features at all (e.g., a block of zeroes).

The block-aligned version has clear performance advantages in terms of both digest generation (the procedure becomes easily parallelizable), and comparison rates (the digests are smaller, approximately 1.6% of the input). Critically, the baseline and the block-aligned versions of the digests are compatible—they can be directly compared without substantial loss of precision and recall. This is true for cases in which the smaller object (the query) is at least 2 KB in size [158].

The baseline (sequential) version of the algorithm is recommended for fingerprinting data objects of up to 16 MiB; larger ones should use the block-aligned version; the sdhash implementation performs this switch automatically.

5.4.4   EVALUATION

One of the critical requirements for any forensic method is that it has well-understood error rates. In the context of approximate matching, the first major hurdle in this process is to *define* what constitutes valid artifact similarity and to develop the means of establishing the ground truth.

The first effort in this area [157], approached the problem from two perspectives: automated controlled tests based on (pseudo-)random data, and manual user evaluation of positive results. The main advantage of controlled experiments is that ground truth is precisely known by construction. Therefore, randomized tests can be run completely automatically and the results be interpreted statistically. The downside is that most real data is not random, so the mapping of experimental results to the general case remains uncertain. Controlled tests are best viewed as characterizing algorithms' baseline capabilities under optimal conditions.

User evaluations offer a more holistic approach in that they capture the process of interpreting the results as seen by an investigator. The problem is that performing such studies is a time consuming process and is inherently limited in scope. Also, it leaves out cases where the byte-level representations of artifacts exhibit similarity, such as the inclusion of boilerplate objects, but the differences are not observable by the user.

Ideally, we want an evaluation method that can *automatically* establish the ground truth for any two artifacts based on a formal definition of similarity. (User evaluations could then be used as a second step, if necessary.)

In the case of byte-wise approximate matching, similarity can be defined in terms of common substrings, or common subsequences. In [16], the authors consider the length of the *longest common substring* (LCS) as the basic measure of similarity. Thus, if the length of LCS is 30% of the length of the shorter string, we can define the similarity as 0.3. Since there can be additional common substrings, LCS is a lower bound on similarity.

From an implementation perspective, LCS is somewhat problematic as the exact solution has quadratic time complexity: $O(|f_1| \times |f_2|)$, where $|f_1|$ and $|f_2|$ are the file lengths, and can be quite large. Coupled with the quadratic growth of the number of comparisons as a function of the number of files in the test set, the exact algorithm quickly becomes impractical. Instead, the proposed solution uses an approximation of LCS, called *aLCS*.

The key idea is to use content-based chunking with a target size of 40 and use the hashes of the resulting chunks to find an approximate lower bound on LCS. Experimental validation on real data shows that, 95% of the time, the aLCS estimate is within 3% of the true value of LCS.

Following the notation from [16], the evaluation methodology can be formalized as follows. Let L_{abs} be the approximated lower bound on the length of the LCS between files f_1 and f_2, as given by aLCS:

$$L_{abs} \quad = \quad alcs(f_1, f_2), \;\; \text{where} \;\; 0 \leq L_{abs} \leq \min(|f_1|, |f_2|).$$

Let L_{rel} be the length of aLCS relative to the size of the shorter file:

$$L_{rel} \quad = \quad \left\lceil 100 \times \frac{L_{abs}}{\min(|f_1|, |f_2|)} \right\rceil, \;\; \text{where} \;\; 0 \leq L_{rel} \leq 100.$$

For a true positive (TP) result, we require that L_{abs} is at least 100 bytes *and* that the relative result L_{rel} exceeds 0.5% of the size of the smaller file. In other words, the true positives/negatives are defined as:

$$
\begin{aligned}
TP_{alcs}(f_1, f_2) &\equiv L_{abs} \geq 100 \;\; \wedge \;\; L_{rel} \geq 1 \\
TN_{alcs}(f_1, f_2) &= \neg TP_{alcs}(f_1, f_2).
\end{aligned}
$$

Let $S_h(f_1, f_2)$ be the result of comparing two files using an approximate matching function h, where $h \in \{ssdeep, sdhash\}$ and $0 \leq S_h \leq 100$. Also, let t be a threshold of significance, which separates matches from non-matches.

Two files, f_1 and f_2, are matched using AM algorithm $h \iff S_h(f_1, f_2) > t$.

$$
\begin{aligned}
TP_h(f_1, f_2, t) &\equiv TP_{alcs}(f_1, f_2) = true \;\; \wedge \;\; S_h(f_1, f_2) > t \\
TN_h(f_1, f_2, t) &\equiv TN_{alcs}(f_1, f_2) = true \;\; \wedge \;\; S_h(f_1, f_2) \leq t \\
FP_h(f_1, f_2, t) &\equiv TN_{alcs}(f_1, f_2) = true \;\; \wedge \;\; S_h(f_1, f_2) > t \\
FN_h(f_1, f_2, t) &\equiv TP_{alcs}(f_1, f_2) = true \;\; \wedge \;\; S_h(f_1, f_2) \leq t.
\end{aligned}
$$

5.5   CLOUD-NATIVE ARTIFACTS

Forensic analysis of cloud systems is still in its infancy but, as discussed in Section 4.6, it will quickly grow in importance. One new and promising avenue is the analysis of *cloud(-native) artifacts*—data objects that maintain the persistent state of web/SaaS applications [163]. Unlike traditional applications, in which the persistent state takes the form of files in the local file system, web apps download the necessary state on the fly and do not rely on local storage.

Recall that a web app's functionality is split between server and client components, and the two communicate over web APIs. From a forensic perspective, the most interesting of the API calls involve (complete) state transfer; for example, opening a document, or loading of a prior version, triggers the transfer of its full content. Conceptually, this is analogous to the process of opening and reading the content of a local file by an application installed on a device. The main difference is that cloud artifacts are *internal* data structures that, unlike a file, are not readily available for analysis.

Cloud artifacts often have a completely different structure from the traditional snapshot-centric encoding. For example, internally, *Google Docs'* documents are represented as the complete history (log) of all editing actions performed on it; given valid credentials, we can obtain this history via the *Google Docs* internal API. It is also possible to obtain a snapshot of the artifact of interest in a standard format, like PDF, via the public API. However, this is *inherently* forensically deficient in that it ignores potentially critical information on the evolution of a document over time (Section 4.6.4).

For the remainder of this section, we will use the analysis of *Google Docs* performed in [163] as a case study illustrating both the new challenges presented by cloud artifacts and the qualitatively new opportunities offered by such efforts.

CASE STUDY: GOOGLE DOCS

Starting in 2007, *Google* initiated an effort to build an online suite of office applications, currently called *G Suite*; individual applications—*Documents, Sheets, Slides*—refer to its constituent document editor, electronic spreadsheet, and slide presentation applications, respectively.

In the 2010 version, the suite was updated with the addition of a document editor supporting online collaboration [81]. The new *Documents* editor, code named *kix*, was "designed specifically for character-by-character real time collaboration using operational transformation"[2][80].

Driven by the overarching requirement for real-time collaboration, *Google* arrived at the conclusion that the simplest approach is to maintain the state as an append-only log of editing actions performed by the users. This has the additional benefit of providing users with fine-grain version history, in which no changes ever get lost. When a specific version is needed, the log is replayed from the beginning until the desired time; replaying the entire log yields the current version.

To support fine-grain revisions, as well as collaborative editing, user actions are pushed to the server as often as every 200 ms, depending on the speed of input. Editing actions performed by different users are merged on the server and a unified history of the document is recorded. When conflicts arise, such as users editing the same word at the same time, the server issues compensatory (or *transformed*) operations such that collaborators end up with the same version of the document.

---

[2]*Operational transformation* is a concurrency management mechanism that eschews preventive locking in favor of reactive, on-the-fly resolution of conflicting user actions by transforming the editing operation to achieve consistency [64].

Changelog

The internal representation of the document, as delivered to the client, is in the form of a JSON object called *changelog*. The structure is nested, containing one array per revision; most elements of the array contain objects (key-value pairs). Each array ends with identifying information for that revision as follows: an epoch timestamp in Unix format, the Google ID of the author, revision number, session ID, session revision number, and the revision itself.

Each time the document is opened, a new session is generated, and the number of revisions that occur within that session are tracked. Some revisions, such as inserting an object, appear as a single entry with multiple actions in the form of a transaction, which contains a series of nested dictionaries. The keys are mneumonic abbreviations (2–8 characters), which aids the analysis.

The changelog contains a special *chunked snapshot* object, which contains all the information needed to create the document as of the starting revision. The length of the snapshot varies greatly depending on the number of embedded *kix* objects and paragraphs; it has only two entries (containing default text styles) for revisions starting at 1.

For any revision with text in the document, the first element of the snapshot consists of a plaintext string of all text in the document, followed by default styles for title, subtitle, and headings *h1* through *h6*, language of the document, and first paragraph index and paragraph styles. The next several elements are all *kix* anchors for embedded objects like comments or suggestions, followed by a listing of each contiguous format area with the styles for those sections that should be applied, as well as paragraphs and associated IDs used to jump to those sections from a table of contents.

Figure 5.3 shows the representation of a minimal example document; one in which the text "Test document" has been typed. In this case, the snapshot (starting on line 3) contains the state of the document before the very last update—the typing of the last three letters: "ent." Thus, the snapshot contains a text insertion for the string "Test docum" (line 4, highlighted), as well as a number of default style definitions and other basic document properties. The log part of the document contains a single insertion of the string "ent" (line 2, highlighted) with the appropriate timestamp and identifying information.

More generally, a document description from revision r_1 to revision r_2 consists of a snapshot of the state at revision r_1, followed by $r_2 - r_1$ entries in the changelog describing each individual change between revisions r_1 and r_2. The ability to choose the range of changes to load, allows *kix* to balance the flexibity of allowing users to go back in time, and the need to be efficient and not replay needlessly ancient document history.

The changelog for a specific range of versions can be obtained manually by using the development tools built into modern browsers. After logging in and opening the document, the list of network requests contains a load URL of the form: `https://docs.google.com/documents/d/<doc_id>/load?<doc_id>&start=<start_rev>&end=<end_rev>&token=<auth_token>`, where `doc_id` is the unique document identifier, `start_rev` is the initial revision (snapshot), `end_rev` the end of the revision range, and `auth_token` is an authentication token (Figure 5.4). The revisions start

```
{"changelog":
   [[{"ty":"is","s":"ent","ibi":11},1453673743519,"04167822183031715453",7,"3581dbee97c438a0",5,null]],
 "chunkedSnapshot":
   [[{"ty":"is","s":"Test docum","ibi":1},
    {"ty":"as","sm":{"hs_h1":{"sdef_ts":{"ts_fs":18.0,"ts_fs_i":false}},
                     "hs_h2":{"sdef_ts":{"ts_fs":14.0,"ts_fs_i":false}},
                     ...
                     "hs_h6":{"sdef_ts":{"ts_bd":false,"ts_bd_i":true,
                        "ts_fgc":"#666666","ts_fgc_i":false,"ts_it":true,"ts_it_i":false}}},
                     "ei":0,"st":"headings","si":0,"fm":false},
    {"ty":"as","sm":{"lgs_l":"en"},"ei":0,"st":"language","si":0,"fm":false},
    {"ty":"as","sm":{"ps_al_i":true,"ps_awao_i":true,"ps_ifl_i":true,"ps_il_i":true,"ps_ir_i":true,
                     "ps_klt_i":true,"ps_kwn_i":true,"ps_ls_i":true,"ps_sa_i":true,"ps_sb_i":true,"ps_sm_i":true},
                     "ei":11,"st":"paragraph","si":11,"fm":false},
    {"ty":"as","sm":{"ts_bd":false, "ts_bd_i":true,"ts_bgc":null,"ts_bgc_i":true,
                     "ts_ff":"Arial","ts_ff_i":true,"ts_fgc":"#000000","ts_fgc_i":true,"ts_fs":11.0,
                     "ts_fs_i":true,"ts_it":false,"ts_it_i":true,"ts_sc":false,"ts_sc_i":true,
                     "ts_st":false,"ts_st_i":true,"ts_un":false,"ts_un_i":true,"ts_va":"nor","ts_va_i":true},
                     "ei":11,"st":"text","si":0,"fm":false}]]}
```

Figure 5.3: *Chunked snapshot* for a document containing the text "Test document" [163].

```
☐ load?id=1IdObEjEPRwAfmYoaSc6vVZVYgrM3oag_mU-Y-3Mj4FQ&start=4943&end=4960&tokcn=AC4w5...

▼ changelog: [[{ty: "mlti", mts: [{ty: "ds", si: 14776, ei: 14776}, {ty: "ds", si: 14775, ei: 14775}]},…],…]
 ▶ 0: [{ty: "mlti", mts: [{ty: "ds", si: 14776, ei: 14776}, {ty: "ds", si: 14775, ei: 14775}]},…]
 ▶ 1: [{ty: "mlti", mts: [{ty: "ds", si: 14774, ei: 14774}, {ty: "is", s: "."}, ibi: 14774}]}, 1443757842902,…]
 ▶ 2: [{ty: "is", s: " ", ibi: 14775}, 1443757843127, "18178839968700900856", 4945, "df36183a2f26250", 660,…]
 ▶ 3: [{ty: "is", s: "Afte", ibi: 14777}, 1443757843660, "18178839968700900856", 4946, "df36183a2f26250",…]
 ▶ 4: [{ty: "is", s: "r a", ibi: 14781}, 1443757843854, "18178839968700900856", 4947, "df36183a2f26250", 662,…]
 ▶ 5: [{ty: "is", s: "n h", ibi: 14784}, 1443757844440, "18178839968700900856", 4948, "df36183a2f26250", 663,…]
 ▶ 6: [{ty: "is", s: "our ", ibi: 14787}, 1443757844751, "18178839968700900856", 4949, "df36183a2f26250",…]
 ▶ 7: [{ty: "is", s: "and ", ibi: 14791}, 1443757845081, "18178839968700900856", 4950, "df36183a2f26250",…]
```

Figure 5.4: Example *load* request and changelog response.

at one and must not exceed the actual number of revisions, and the start cannot be greater than the end.

Embedded Images

Inserting an image into the document produces a URL in the changelog from the `googleusercontent.com` domain—Google's content distribution network (CDN)—where a copy of the image is hosted. The link is publicly accessible to anyone with the correct URL (which is long and appears random). To handle image data, the (internal) *Documents* API has a `renderdata` method. It is used with a POST request with the same headers and query strings as the `load` method used to fetch the changelog: `https://docs.google.com/document/d/<doc_id>/renderdata?id=<doc_id>`. The `renderdata` request body contains a bulk data request in the form:

```
renderOps:{"r0":["image",{"cosmoId":"1dv ... cRQ",
                          "container":"1Ss ... xps"}],
           "r1":["image",{"cosmoId":"1xv ... 3df",
                          "container":"1Ss ... xps"}],
      ...
}
```

The `cosmoId` values observed correspond to the `i_cid` attribute of embedded pictures in the changelog, and the `container` is the document id. The `renderdata` response contains a list of the CDN-hosted URLs that are world readable.

One side effect of the *Documents* artifact model is that an embedded image remains available from the CDN as long as *at least one revision* of a document references it. This behavior is the result of keeping the complete version history, which implies that the user has the option to go back to *any* version of the document; thus, the system must maintain a live copy of the data until all references are deleted (at which point it becomes available for garbage collection). Forensically, this is an interesting behavior that could uncover very old data, long considered destroyed by its owners.

Reverting to a previous version does *not* destroy the editing history of the document; instead, a *revert* operations containing a snapshot of the desired new state is added to the history. In other words, the *reversion* operation itself can be later walked back and the state before it can be examined, consistent with the append-only design chosen by Google.

Slides

The *Slides* app uses a similar changelog approach to transfer the state of the artifacts—the data is communicated as an abstract data structure, which is intepreted and rendered by the JavaScript client code. The overall formatting of the log is similar, but is encoded as an array of arrays and values (in effect, a tuple)—instead of a hash map and values. This makes the reverse engineering a bit more cumbersome, but it does not change the overall analytical approach.

Adding a slide consists of a group of operations (a transaction) containing the creation of a slide, setting of slide attributes, and insertion of text boxes (based on the template). Duplicating a slide is a large transaction, consisting of the creation of the same slide type, and—for each text box on old slide—the addition of a box, as well as the respective text and style. Deletion is another transaction, where each box is deleted from the slide first, followed by the slide itself. Changing the theme of a slide creates a massive number of actions inside a transaction with an entirely new slide being created, and each text box is created and has 30–40 modification actions associated with it, followed by the old slide having all of its text boxes deleted and, finally, the old slide itself deleted.

Suggestions and Comments

Suggestions are marked up edits to the document that can be accepted, or rejected, by the collaborators; this is similar to the "track changes" mode in *Microsoft Word*. They are present in the changelog and are treated similarly to other changes; however, they have dedicated operation types that allow the editor to treat them differently in terms of formatting and UI (Figure 5.5).

```
▼ changelog: [,…]
  ▶ 0: [{ty: "dss", si: 85, ei: 98}, 1444094632128, "18178839968700900856", 174, "49d79c9f90192ecb", 135,…]
  ▶ 1: [{ty: "mlti", mts: [{ty: "iss", sugid: "suggest.uzuelc2xg0i", s: "n", ibi: 85},…]}, 1444094636436,…]
  ▶ 2: [{ty: "iss", sugid: "suggest.uzuelc2xg0i", s: "e", ibi: 86}, 1444094637189, "18178839968700900856",…]
  ▶ 3: [{ty: "iss", sugid: "suggest.uzuelc2xg0i", s: "w", ibi: 87}, 1444094637807, "18178839968700900856",…]
  ▶ 4: [{ty: "iss", sugid: "suggest.uzuelc2xg0i", s: " ", ibi: 88}, 1444094640910, "18178839968700900856",…]
```

Figure 5.5: Suggestion changelog example (truncated).

Comments are not explicitly represented in the changelog; instead, a *kix* anchor id is present (Figure 5.6). The Google Drive API has a *list* method, which allows the retrieval of all comments associated with a document, including deleted ones. However, the actual content of deleted comments is stripped away; only current and resolved ones are retrievable in full.

```
▼ changelog: [,…]
  ▼ 0: [{ty: "as", sm: {das a: {cv: {op: "insert", opIndex: 0, opValue: "kix.p5y4wk55ms36"}}}, ei: 128,…},…]
    ▼ 0: {ty: "as", sm: {das a: {cv: {op: "insert", opIndex: 0, opValue: "kix.p5y4wk55ms36"}}}, ei: 128,…}
        ei: 128
        fm: false
        si: 115
      ▶ sm: {das a: {cv: {op: "insert", opIndex: 0, opValue: "kix.p5y4wk55ms36"}}}
        st: "doco anchor"
        ty: "as"
    1: 1444094979511
```

Figure 5.6: Comment changelog example (truncated).

CHAPTER 6

Open Issues and Challenges

6.1   SCALABILITY

Although the first discussions on the foreseen need for scalable architectures for forensic process-ing date back to 2004 [150, 166], the issue has become a top-level *practical* concern over the last 3–4 years. The need is most easily motivated by observing three core trends: (a) The size and com-plexity of forensic targets will continue to grow at an exponential rate for the foreseable future; (b) Human resources charged with the problem will not grow appreciably, relative to the expected data growth; (c) There are real-world deadlines to any digital forensic analysis, which means that turnaround time must remain stable, despite the expected data growth and growing data load per forensic expert.

Put together, these observations point to the need to develop forensic processing systems that can scale out in order to match the growing demand with a comparable increase in hardware resources. We refer to this property as *data scalability* [156] and there are hardly any systems that provide complete solutions. The *Hansken* project at the *Neatherlands Forensic Institute* [94, 188] comes closest to fulfilling that vision on the basis of commodity big data technology.

The ultimate measure of a solution's data scalability is maintaining constant processing times in the face of ever growing processing demands. We discussed this in Section 4.4.2, which argued that forensic processing ought to be viewed as a *real-time* task.

Another aspect of scalability is *cost*—the ability to grow processing capacity on a fixed annual budget. This is where Moore's Law helps (despite its slowing growth and predictions of its imminent demise) by promising increases in CPU capacity per unit of cost.

Extensibility—the ability to incrementally accommodate new functional modules into the forensic flow at (near) zero cost—is also an important component of the needed solution, as it enables the analysis of new types of evidence to match the increasing diversity of forensic targets.

6.2   VISUALIZATION AND COLLABORATION

It should be clear that scalability is a necessary, but not a sufficient condition to meet investigation deadlines: it does not address the additional load on the investigator. For example, the ability to index data 10 times faster means that we could process a target 10 times larger in the same amount of time, but this would also result in the investigator having to go through that much more evidence.

One component of the solution that is currently not widely employed is the use of advanced visual analytics to aggregate, present, explore, and query the available evidence. This would be an important and necessary improvement in the ability of investigators to manage larger cases. We should recognize, however, that visualization provides a one-time gain and, over the long run, does not (on its own) address the information overload of the analyst.

Another incremental component of the solution is embedded support for collaboration, which would allow a team of investigators to *effectively* and *efficiently* work together on a large case, or one of higher priority. In addition to the ability to pool human resources, collaboration support opens up the possibility of improved investigative processes by, for example, allowing the development of specialized skills, and the seamless integration of team members of different levels of expertise.

6.3   AUTOMATION AND INTELLIGENCE

Despite the fact that relatively little work has been done in the area, visualization and collaboration should be viewed as the low-hanging fruit in terms of improving the efficiency of analysts; they will certainly not be enough.

The main source of sustained improvement will be the development of ever higher levels of automation and abstraction of the forensic processing. This means automated identification of facts and automated reasoning about the facts at abstraction levels that approach the ones used by analysts. Clearly, the development of such capabilities will take a substantial amount of time and effort but, arguably, they will be of the highest long-term significance to the future of digital forensic analysis.

6.4   PERVASIVE ENCRYPTION

One of the most consequential technology developments over the last three decades is the introduction and widespread use of encryption techniques to ensure the confidentiality and integrity of data and communications. The main drivers of this development have been the pervasive digitization of almost all data storage and transmission. This led to the need to adopt new means of controlling access to information, and encryption plays a central role in this process.

In the early days of modern digital forensics (the 1980s) the use of encryption was restricted to, and tightly contolled by, government agencies. The 1991 publication of the PGP cryptosystem [8, 21] by Phil Zimmermann marks the first serious effort to make encryption readily available to the individual computer user. A year later, *Netscape* introduced SSL (originally RFC 2246, successively deprecated by RFC 6176 and 7568) in its web browser, thereby providing the first mass means for encrypted communication over the Internet. As of 2016, sophisticated, open-source encryption software is widely available throughout the world, and law enforcement agencies encounter serious problems accessing the plaintext version of enrypted data found during investigations.

Conceptually, there are two approaches to cryptanalysis: find flaws with the encryption *method* or attack its *implementation*. Successful method attacks of early methods were relatively easy; however, the field has quickly grown and matured; the main focus today is on attacking the implementation, that is, finding exploitable software bugs.

Although access to plaintext data is a necessary prerequisite for forensic analysis, our contention is that cryptanalysis, *per se*, should not be considered a core forensic concern. By definition, if a strong cryptosystem (with no known mathematical deficiencies) is properly implemented, it must not be possible to obtain the plaintext without the key. Since individual and societal trust in the cyber infrastructure is predicated on strong (encryption-based) security and privacy mechanisms, it is logical to expect that those will be reconciled with the need to perform forensic data examinations via the legal system. This is not to suggest that available attacks should not be applied for forensic purposes, but that digital forensic researchers should focus on other critical problems, of which there is no shortage.

At present, one very useful approach to deal with encryption is to get *around* it by extracting the relevant key from the available data. This is commonly feasible if a memory snapshot of the computation employing encryption is available. For example, *mimikatz* [51, 52] is one tool specializing in the extraction of a variety of security credentials from RAM. Although the targeted software could try to tweak its implementation to make the extraction difficult, it cannot prevent it with certainty.

This opportunity to perform key extraction from RAM, where data tends to be in plaintext, is likely to be closed in the foreseeable future. The impetus for this comes from the legitimate concerns of cloud customers who currently have to completely trust their cloud provider not to compromise their most sensitive data, such as encryption keys. *Intel*'s *Software Guard Extensions* (Intel SGX) [5] is a CPU technology that allows select code and data to be protected from disclosure, or modification, by means of software containers called *enclaves*. Inside the enclave, software's code, data, and stack are protected by hardware-enforced access control policies that prevent attacks against the enclave's content. This means that sensitive encryption/decryption routines, and associated keys, will soon become inaccessible for analysis.

6.5   CLOUD COMPUTING

Section 4.6 already discussed some of the emerging issues and some early experiences in working with cloud forensic targets. Here we provide a brief discussion of the underlying trends, and use it to outline some of the issues that forensic tools will need to address.

6.5.1   FROM SAAP TO SAAS

As already discussed, the fundamental change taking place in IT is the fast, ongoing transition from *Software as a Product* (SaaP) to *Software as a Service* (SaaS). This is not only a technological shift, but also a wholesale change in the way software is developed, delivered, and maintained. Of particular consequence to forensics is the accompanying change of ownership and management of code and data:

No physicial media acquisition. The idea of acquiring data from original physical media, and indepedently rebuilding the logical data structures, such as files, from first principles, is completely unworkable. From an ownership perspective, physical media is first aggregated (using RAID), and then finely, and dynamically allocated to different users and uses (with a sanitization step between allocations). Another means by which customers (implicitly) share physical resources is databases, which may contain records from numerous applications. NIST Working Group's report [133] enumerates 65 different challenges to cloud forensics; most are a direct consequence of the effort to literally apply existing SaaP methods to a SaaS world.

Code is unobservable. Investigating a product allows for the software of interest to be installed under contolled conditions, and its functions systematically mapped using differential analysis techniques [75]. It is also possible to examine the machine code and explicitly reverse engineer the functionality.

Web applications are split between a thin client (constisting of minified and/or obfuscated *Javascript*) and server-side code, accessed over one, or more, service APIs. Clearly, service implementations are not readily available for inspection and controlled experimentation.

One more complication is that, for performance reasons, the amount of processing may shift dynamically between the client and server components. For example, the service may switch from delivering abstract data structures in JSON, to be processed and rendered by the client, to delivering straight up HTML to be rendered directly by the browser.

Data at rest is not directly observable. Web apps (SaaS) receive the data they need to work with the user *on demand* over the network; local storage may be used for performance-related caching, or to survive temporary network outages. Complete visibility is not guaranteed even for cloud storage services, like *Dropbox* and *Google Drive*, which are explicitly designed to work with user-defined data: not all data may be replicated to the client, and historical versions are not available locally [161]. In sum, locally cached data provides a record that is incomplete, of unknown provenance, and in proprietary data formats that may change at any time.

6.5.2   SEPARATING CLOUD SERVICES FROM THEIR IMPLEMENTATION

The complimentary step in understanding the problem is to separate the concept of the cloud—the seemless and scalable delivery of computational services—from its currently common implementation technology—the use of hardware virtualization.

It is natural in this transitional period to look for similarities between traditional physical device forensics and that of cloud environments. The latter are commonly classified into SaaS, PaaS, and IaaS: software-, platform-, and infrastructure-as-a-service, respectively. At present, an IaaS deployment looks a lot like a network of machines, only virtual, with identifiable CPU, RAM, and storage components.

It is tempting to assume that simply applying existing techniques solves the problem and that nothing substantive has changed. It would also be wrong, and two main points are relevant:

The true purpose of the cloud is SaaS. For the vast majority of organizations, the main point is not to switch from managing physical machines to managing virtual ones, but to stop even thinking about the IT infrastructure as anything more than another utility bill to pay. This means that organizations are ultimately looking for a complete SaaS solution, and this will often involve multiple layers of providers. The Cisco's Global Cloud Index Report [38] projects that, by 2019, the majority of cloud workloads will be SaaS, while the share of IaaS will shrink. IaaS services will still be needed but those services will be used by other providers that will build the rest of the software stack and provide users with a complete service solution. Investigating the whole stack would be prohibitively complicated from both technology and legal standpoints. Therefore, the main problem faced by forensics will be the investigation of SaaS, not IaaS.

The cloud implementation stack is evolving. After working through the initial growing pains, both service providers and customers have relentlessly focused on driving down the operating costs by optimizing the efficiency of the implementation and by simplifying the development environment. The movement to *container* environments, based on OS-level virtualization mechanisms, can slim down the deployment stack and improve the overall efficiency of the system.

Using tools like Docker (docker.org), containerized software can be deployed in bespoke minimal configurations consisting only of system libraries and services needed. Attempting to investigate the implementations of such environments would be legally problematic and would scale poorly as each deployment would have to be examined from scratch.

Amazon's *AWS Lambda* [4, 9] goes further along this path—it offers the hosting of individual pieces of code (functions) without the need to build and maintain an operating environment. The idea is to provide a platform that allows clients to write event handling functions that require no explicit provisioning of resources on the part of the customer.

6.5.3   RESEARCH CHALLENGES

Big log analysis. The cloud brings true big data challenges and opportunities to learn from other domains. The good news is that most of the forensically interesting data will be recorded explicitly in event logs maintained by the various components of the cloud system. The challenge will be to find the nuggets of relevent information inside the mountains of data.

Automated API analysis. We are still early in the cloud era of computing and, for the foreseeable future, we should expect the number and variety of cloud services to continue to grow at a fast rate. Based on observations from prior development cycles, we can expect similar services to appear in numerous competing implementations. This creates a major problem for forensic software to keep up with all the new developments and presents an interesting research challenge to develop automated means to understand API semantics and generate code to acquire and analyze data acquired via APIs.

Forward deployment. Based on current hardware trends, it is safe to predict that, within the next 5–10 years, the vast majority of the data will be generated, hosted, and processed in the cloud. Cloud providers are actively encouraging the accumulation of data on their infrastructure by providing free upload bandwidth and cheap long-term storage. Eventually, the sheer volume of data will make it impractical—for both performance and cost reasons—to perform forensic acquisitions over the network. The logical solution is to forward-deploy the forensic processing suite and execute the performance-critical portion of the analysis on the provider's infrastructure.

6.6   INTERNET OF THINGS (IOT)

At present, the term IoT is defined somewhat vaguely but it generally refers to networks of connected devices designed to sustain cyber-physical processes. As per NIST's SP 800-183 [190], such systems consists of several types of primitives:

- *sensor*—a utility, which measures physical properties of the environment, such as temperature, pressure, and acceleration;

- *aggregator*—a software implementation of a mathematical function that produces intermediate, aggregated data, such as averages;

- *communication channel*—a medium by which data is transmitted between sensing, computing, and actuation components, e.g., USB, Ethernet, wireless;

- *eUtility*—or *external utility* is a software or hardware product, or service, such as a cloud;

- *decision trigger*—creates the final result(s) needed to satisfy the purpose, specification, and requirements of a specific network of things, e.g., control an actuator, or produce a prediction.

The architectures of individual systems will vary but most implementations are expected to have all of the above components; the implementation may bundle some of them together. For example, an autonomous UAV is a highly integrated platform, whereas embedded enviromental sensors (such as temperature) could be part of multiple networks of things. From a forensic perspective, an integrated system (such as a drone) looks similar to a general purposes compute system, so traditional forenic methods are likely to be effective. The more distributed implementations will present a somewhat different set of challenges.

Many devices will not be available for physical inspection. They will be embedded in the environment and will be packaged as disposable items not designed to be serviced. More importantly, they will have extremely limited (if any) abilities to retain data.

Computations are ephemeral. The AWS Lambda computational model is likely to dominate—it is very easy to construct simple processing pipelines that can automatically be scaled by the infrastructure. There will be no leftover artifacts beyond what is explicitly recorded by the handler code.

Historical data will likely be deposited in the cloud. All storage and computational resources will be on the server end, and no intermediate (cached) data is likely to be retained. IoT gateways may be the only exception, but the amount of data retained is likely to be relatively small.

Therefore, the main forensic target is likely to be the *eUtility* where we can expect the vast majority of historical data to reside. It would be logical to assume that most *eUtility* implementations will be backed by a cloud service, so corresponding methods and tools developed for cloud forensics should remain relevant.

Bibliography

[1] 18 US Code § 1030 - Fraud and related activity in connection with computers. `https://www.law.cornell.edu/uscode/text/18/1030` 5

[2] AccessData. Description of products. Archived: Dec 16, 1996. 5

[3] Amazon. Announcing amazon elastic compute cloud (amazon EC2)—beta. `https://aws.amazon.com/about-aws/whats-new/2006/08/24/announcing-amazon-elastic-compute-cloud-amazon-ec2---beta/` 6

[4] Amazon. AWS Lambda—serverless compute. `https://aws.amazon.com/lambda/` 121

[5] Anati, I., Gueron, S., Johnson, S., and Scarlata, V. Innovative technology for CPU based attestation and sealing. In *Proc. of the 2nd Workshop on Hardware and Architectural Support for Security and Privacy (HASP)*, 2013. `https://software.intel.com/sites/default/files/article/413939/hasp-2013-innovative-technology-for-attestation-and-sealing.pdf` 119

[6] Apple. Apple reinvents the phone with iPhone. `https://www.apple.com/pr/library/2007/01/09Apple-Reinvents-the-Phone-with-iPhone.html` 7

[7] Ashton, K. That "internet of things" thing, 2009. `http://www.rfidjournal.com/articles/view?4986` 7

[8] Atkins, D., Stallings, W., and Zimmermann, P. PGP message exchange formats, 1996. RFC 1991. DOI: 10.17487/rfc1991. 118

[9] Barr, J. AWS Lambda—run code in the cloud, 2014. `https://aws.amazon.com/blogs/aws/run-code-cloud/` 7, 121

[10] Becher, M., Dornseif, M., and Klein, C. FireWire all your memory are belong to us. In *5th Annual CanSecWest Conference*, 2005. `https://cansecwest.com/core05/2005-firewire-cansecwest.pdf` 65

[11] Berger, M. *Reference Manual on Scientific Evidence*, 3rd ed., National Academies Press, 2011, ch. The Admissibility of Expert Testimony, pp. 11–36. `http://www2.fjc.gov/sites/default/files/2012/SciMan3D01.pdf` DOI: 10.17226/13163. 9

[12] Berners-Lee, T. and L. M. Uniform resource locators (url), 1994. RFC 1738. DOI: 10.17487/rfc1738. 36

126   BIBLIOGRAPHY

[13] Beverly, R., Garfinkel, S., and Cardwell, G.   Forensic carving of network packets and associated data structures.   In *Proc. of the 11th Annual DFRWS Conference. DFRWS'11.*, 2011, pp. S78–S89. DOI: 10.1016/j.diin.2011.05.010. 56

[14] Bloom, B. H. Space/time trade-offs in hash coding with allowable errors. *Communications of ACM 13*, 7, July 1970, pp. 422–426. DOI: 10.1145/362686.362692. 101

[15] Breitinger, F., Guttman, B., McCarrin, M., and Roussev, V.   Approximate matching: Definition and terminology.   DRAFT NIST Special Publication 800-168.   DOI: 10.6028/nist.sp.800-168. 103

[16] Breitinger, F. and Roussev, V. Automated evaluation of approximate matching algorithms on real data. In *Proc. of the 1st Annual Digital Forensic Research Conference Europe (DFRWS-EU)*, 2014, pp. S10–S17. DOI: 10.1016/j.diin.2014.03.002. 109, 110

[17] Broder, A. On the resemblance and containment of documents. In *Compression and Complexity of Sequences*, Jun 1997, pp. 21–29. DOI: 10.1109/sequen.1997.666900. 103

[18] Broder, A. and Mitzenmatcher, M. Network applications of Bloom filters: A survey. *Internet Mathematics*, 4, 2002, pp. 485–509. DOI: 10.1080/15427951.2004.10129096. 101

[19] Burdach, M. Physical memory forensics. In *BlackHat Europe*, 2006. `https://www.blackhat.com/presentations/bh-usa-06/BH-US-06-Burdach.pdf` 65

[20] Calhoun, W. and Coles, D.   Predicting the types of file fragments.   In *The Proc. of the 8th Annual DFRWS Conference. DFRWS'08*, 2008, pp. S14–S20. DOI: 10.1016/j.diin.2008.05.005. 60

[21] Callas, J., Donnerhacke, L., Finney, H., Shaw, D., and Thayer, R.   OpenPGP message format, 2007.   RFC 4880. DOI: 10.17487/rfc4880. 118

[22] Carrier, B.   The sleuthkit (tsk) and autopsy: Open source digital forensics tools. `http://sleuthkit.org` 41

[23] Carrier, B.   *File System Forensic Analysis*, 1st ed.,   Addison-Wesley Professional, 2005. ISBN: 978-0321268174. 2, 6, 44, 48, 50, 51, 52

[24] Carrier, B., Casey, E., and Venema, W. DFRWS 2006 Forensics Challenge, 2006. `http://old.dfrws.org/2006/challenge/index.shtml` 55

[25] Carrier, B., Casey, E., and Venema, W. DFRWS 2007 Forensics Challenge, 2007. `http://old.dfrws.org/2007/challenge/index.shtml` 55

[26] Carrier, B. and Grand, J.   A hardware-based memory acquisition procedure for digital investigations.   *Journal of Digital Investigation 1*, 1, 2004, pp. 50–60. DOI: 10.1016/j.diin.2003.12.001. 65

[27] Carrier, B. and Spafford, E. Categories of digital investigation analysis techniques based on the computer history model. In *Proc. of the 2005 Digital Forensic Research Conference (DFRWS)*, 2006, pp. S121–S130. DOI: 10.1016/j.diin.2006.06.011. 16, 17, 18, 22

[28] Carvey, H. Forensic scanner, 2012. `https://github.com/appliedsec/forensicscan ner` 77

[29] Carvey, H. *Windows Forensic Analysis Toolkit: Advanced Analysis Techniques for Windows 8*, 4th ed., Syngress, 2014. ISBN: 978-0124171572. 2

[30] Carvey, H. *Windows Registry Forensics: Advanced Digital Forensic Analysis of the Windows Registry*, 2nd ed., Syngress, 2016. ISBN: 978-0128032916. 2

[31] Case, A. and III, G. G. R. Detecting objective-c malware through memory forensics. In *Proc. of the 16th Annual Digital Forensic Research Conference (DFRWS)*, 2016, pp. S3–S10. DOI: 10.1016/j.diin.2016.04.017. 70

[32] Casey, E. *Digital Evidence and Computer Crime: Forensic Science, Computers and the Internet*, 3rd ed., Academic Press, 2011. ISBN: 978-0123742681. 2

[33] Comprehensive crime control act of 1984. `https://www.ncjrs.gov/App/publicatio ns/Abstract.aspx?id=123365` 5

[34] Cesare, S. Runtime kernel kmem patching, 1998. `http://althing.cs.dartmouth.e du/local/vsc07.html` 65

[35] Chen, P., Lee, E., Gibson, G., Katz, R., and Patterson, D. Raid: High-performance, reliable secondary storage. *ACM Computing Surveys 26*, 2, Jun 1994, pp. 145–185. DOI: 10.1145/176979.176981. 39, 41

[36] Chow, J., Pfaff, B., Garfinkel, T., Christopher, K., and Rosenblum, M. Understanding data lifetime via whole system simulation. In *Proc. of the USENIX Security Symposium*, 2004, pp. 321–336. `https://www.usenix.org/legacy/publications/library/pro ceedings/sec04/tech/chow/chow_html/` 62

[37] Chung, H., Park, J., Lee, S., and Kang, C. Digital forensic investigation of cloud storage services. *Journal of Digital Investigation 9*, 2, 2012, pp. 81–95. DOI: 10.1016/j.diin.2012.05.015. 81

[38] Cisco. Cisco global cloud index: Forecast and methodology, 2013–2018 (updated Nov 2014). `http://www.cisco.com/c/en/us/solutions/collateral/service-provid er/global-cloud-index-gci/Cloud_Index_White_Paper.pdf` 121

[39] Cohen, M. The PyFlag Wiki. Archived (Dec 22, 2011). `https://web.archive.org/ web/20111229063058/http://www.pyflag.net/` 71

[40] Cohen, M. PyFlag—An advanced network forensic framework. In *Proc. of the 8th Annual Digital Forensic Research Conference (DFRWS)*, 2008, pp. S112–S120. DOI: 10.1016/j.diin.2008.05.016. 71

[41] Cohen, M., Garfinkel, S., and Schatz, B. Extending the advanced forensic format to accommodate multiple data sources, logical evidence, arbitrary information and forensic workflow. In *Proc. of the 9th Annual Digital Forensic Research Conference (DFRWS)*, 2009, pp. S57–S68. DOI: 10.1016/j.diin.2009.06.010. 36, 37, 38

[42] Cohen, M., Sindelar, A., Moser, A., Stuettgen, J., Sanchez, J., and Bushkov, M. Rekall forensic, 2015. http://www.rekall-forensic.com/ 69

[43] Cohen, M. I. In *Characterization of the windows kernel version variability for accurate memory analysis*, 2015, pp. S38–S49. DOI: 10.1016/j.diin.2015.01.009. 69

[44] Compaq Computer Corp., Phoenix Technologies Ltd., and Intel Corp. Bios boot specification (version 1.01), 1996. https://www.phoenix.com/resources/specs-bbs101.pdf 43, 61

[45] CompuServe. Graphics Interchange Format(sm), Version 89a. http://www.w3.org/Graphics/GIF/spec-gif89a.txt 5

[46] Corey, V., Peterman, C., Shearin, S., Greenberg, M., and Bokkelen, J. V. Network forensics analysis. *IEEE Internet Computing 6*, 6, Nov 2002, pp. 60–66. DOI: 10.1109/mic.2002.1067738. 71

[47] Western Digital Corp. WD Green desktop hard drives, drive specification sheet, 2014. http://www.droboworks.com/datasheets/Hard-Drives/WD-Green-Desktop-Specsheet.pdf 75

[48] Western Digital Corp. WD Black desktop hard drives, drive specification sheet, 2015. https://www.wdc.com/content/dam/wdc/website/downloadable_assets/eng/spec_data_sheet/2879-771434.pdf 75

[49] Intel Corporation. Intel 64 and IA-32 architectures software developer's manual, 2011. https://www.wdc.com/content/dam/wdc/website/downloadable_assets/eng/spec_data_sheet/2879-771434.pdf 68

[50] Cruz, F., Moser, A., and Cohen, M. A scalable file based data store for forensic analysis. In *Proc. of the 2nd Annual DFRWS Europe (DFRWS-EU)*, 2015, pp. S90–S101. DOI: 10.1016/j.diin.2015.01.016. 39

[51] Delpy, B. mimikatz 2.0, 2014. http://blog.gentilkiwi.com/downloads/mimikatz-rmll.pdf 119

[52] Delpy, B. mimikatz: A little tool to play with Windows security, 2016. `https://github.com/gentilkiwi/mimikatz` 119

[53] DFRWS. DFRWS 2005 forensics challenge, 2005. `http://old.dfrws.org/2005/challenge/index.shtml` 6

[54] Dolan-Gavitt, B. The VAD tree: A process-eye view of physical memory. In *Proc. of the 7th Annual Digital Forensic Research Conference (DFRWS)*, 2007, pp. 62–64. DOI: 10.1016/j.diin.2007.06.008. 70

[55] Dolan-Gavitt, B. Forensic analysis of the windows registry in memory. In *Proc. of the 8th Annual Digital Forensic Research Conference (DFRWS)*, 2008, pp. S26–S32. DOI: 10.1016/j.diin.2008.05.003. 70

[56] Dolan-Gavitt, B., Srivastava, A., Traynor, P., and Giffin, J. Robust signatures for kernel data structures. In *Proc. of the 16th ACM Conference on Computer and Communications Security*, New York, NY, 2009, ACM, pp. 566–577. DOI: 10.1145/1653662.1653730. 69

[57] Drago, I., Bocchi, E., Mellia, M., Slatman, H., and Pras, A. Benchmarking personal cloud storage. In *Proc. of the 2013 Conference on Internet Measurement Conference*, 2013, pp. 205–212. DOI: 10.1145/2504730.2504762. 82

[58] Drago, I., Mellia, M., Munafo, M., Sperotto, A., Sadre, R., and Pras, A. Inside dropbox: Understanding personal cloud storage services. In *Proc. of the 2012 ACM Conference on Internet Measurement Conference*, 2012, pp. 481–494. DOI: 10.1145/2398776.2398827. 82

[59] Dropbox. Dropbox API v2: Build your app on the Dropbox platform, 2016. `https://www.dropbox.com/developers` 94

[60] Dutch National Police Agency. CarvFS user space file-system for usage with zero-storage (in-place) carving tools. `https://github.com/DNPA/carvfs` 55, 95

[61] Dykstra, J. and Sherman, A. Understanding issues in cloud forensics: Two hypothetical case studies. In *Proc. of the ADFSL Conference on Digital Forensics, Security and Law*, 2011, pp. 45–54. `http://proceedings.adfsl.org/index.php/CDFSL/article/view/74/72` 84

[62] Dykstra, J. and Sherman, A. T. Acquiring forensic evidence from infrastructure-as-a-service cloud computing: Exploring and evaluating tools, trust, and techniques. In *The Proc. of the 12th Annual Digital Forensics Research Conference (DFRWS)*, 2012, pp. S90–S98. DOI: 10.1016/j.diin.2012.05.001. 87

[63] Dykstra, J. and Sherman, A. T.   Design and implementation of FROST: Digital forensic tools for the OpenStack cloud computing platform.   In *Proc. of the 13th Annual Digital Forensics Research Conference (DFRWS)*, 2013, pp. S87–S95. DOI: 10.1016/j.diin.2013.06.010. 87, 89

[64] Ellis, C. and Gibbs, S. Concurrency control in groupware systems. In *Proc. of the 1989 ACM SIGMOD International Conference on Management of Data*, 1989, pp. 399–407. DOI: 10.1145/67544.66963. 111

[65] Foundation, V. Volatility framework, 2007–2015. `https://github.com/volatilityf oundation/volatility/` 69

[66] Frederick, P. and Brooks, J. The computer scientist as toolsmith ii. *Communications of the ACM 39*, 3, Mar 1996, pp. 61–68. DOI: 10.1145/227234.227243. 1

[67] Free Software Foundation. Ddrescue—data recovery tool, 2015. `https://www.gnu.or g/software/ddrescue/` 32

[68] FreeBSD. dd(1) FreeBSD general commands manual, 2014. `https://www.freebsd.or g/cgi/man.cgi?query=dd(1)` 32

[69] Fridrich, J. and Goljan, M. Robust hash functions for digital watermarking. In *Proc. of the International Conference on Information Technology: Coding and Computing*, 2000, pp. 178–183. DOI: 10.1109/itcc.2000.844203. 104

[70] Garfinkel, S. Network forensics: Tapping the internet. `http://archive.oreilly.com/ pub/a/network/2002/04/26/nettap.html` 71

[71] Garfinkel, S. Carving contiguous and fragmented files with fast object validation. In *Proc. of the 2007 DFRWS Conference*, 2007, pp. S2–S12. DOI: 10.1016/j.diin.2007.06.017. 55

[72] Garfinkel, S. Digital forensics research: The next 10 years. In *Proc. of the 2010 DFRWS Conference*, 2010. DOI: 10.1016/j.diin.2010.05.009. 5, 6

[73] Garfinkel, S., Malan, D., Dubec, K.-A., Stevens, C., and Pham, C. *Advanced Forensic Format: An Open Extensible Format for Disk Imaging*. Springer New York, Boston, MA, 2006, pp. 13–27. DOI: 10.1007/0-387-36891-4_2. 34

[74] Garfinkel, S., Nelson, A., White, D., and Roussev, V. Using purpose-built functions and block hashes to enable small block and sub-file forensics. In *Proc. of the 10th Annual DFRWS Conference. DFRWS'10.*, 2010. DOI: 10.1016/j.diin.2010.05.003. 57, 100

[75] Garfinkel, S., Nelson, A. J., and Young, J. A general strategy for differential forensic analysis. In *12th Annual Digital Forensics Research Conference*, 2012, pp. S50–S59. DOI: 10.1016/j.diin.2012.05.003. 13, 14, 15, 120

[76] Geiger, M., Venema, W., and Casey, E. DFRWS 2008 forensics challenge, 2008. `http://old.dfrws.org/2008/challenge/index.shtml` 6

[77] Goodspeed, T.   Some practical thoughts concerning active disk antiforensics, 2014.   *Keynote Address, 14th Annual Digital Forensic Conference (DFRWS'14)*. `http://www.dfrws.org/sites/default/files/session-files/pres-some_practical_thoughts_concerning_active_disk_antiforensics.pdf` 32

[78] Goodstein, D. *Reference Manual on Scientific Evidence*, 3rd ed., National Academies Press, 2011, ch. The Admissibility of Expert Testimony, pp. 37–54. `http://www2.fjc.gov/sites/default/files/2012/SciMan3D01.pdf` 9

[79] Google. Google gets the message, launches gmail. `http://googlepress.blogspot.com/2004/04/google-gets-message-launches-gmail.html` 6

[80] Google. Google drive blog archive, May 2010. `http://googledrive.blogspot.com/2010_05_01_archive.html` 111

[81] Google. The next generation of google docs, 2010. `http://googleblog.blogspot.com/2010/04/next-generation-of-google-docs.html` 111

[82] Google. Google drive API v3: Download files, 2016. `https://developers.google.com/drive/v3/web/manage-downloads` 93

[83] Guidance Software. Tableau td2 forensic 1:2 duplicator. `https://guidancesoftware.com/products/Pages/tableau/products/forensic-duplicators/td2.aspx` 33

[84] Guidance Software. Encase evidence file format version 2, 2012. Technical Specification. `https://www.guidancesoftware.com/resources/Pages/doclib/Document-Library/EnCase-Evidence-File-Format-Version-2.aspx` 33, 35

[85] Hale, J. Amazon cloud drive forensic analysis. *Journal of Digital Investigation 10*, October 2013, pp. 295–265. DOI: 10.1016/j.diin.2013.04.006. 81

[86] Hand, S., Lin, Z., Gu, G., and Thuraisingham, B. Bin-carver: Automatic recovery of binary executable files. In *The Proc. of the 2012 DFRWS Conference*, 2012, pp. S108–S117. DOI: 10.1016/j.diin.2012.05.014. 56

[87] Harbour, N. dcfldd, 2006. `http://dcfldd.sourceforge.net/` 32

[88] Harrell, C. Overall df investigation process, 2010. `http://journeyintoir.blogspot.com/2010/10/overall-df-investigation-process.html` 74

[89] Hasan, R., Sion, R., and Winslett, M. Introducing secure provenance: Problems and challenges. In *Proc. of the 2007 ACM Workshop on Storage Security and Survivability*, New York, NY, 2007, pp. 13–18. DOI: 10.1145/1314313.1314318. 88

[90] Henk, C. and Szeredi, M. Filesystem in userspace. `http://fuse.sourceforge.net/` 55, 95

[91] Heydari, M. M. H. Content based file type detection algorithms. In *Proc. of the 36th Annual Hawaii International Conference on System Sciences (HICCS'03)*, 2003, IEEE Computer Society. DOI: 10.1109/hicss.2003.1174905. 59

[92] Ho, A. and Li, S., Eds. *Handbook of Digital Forensics of Multimedia Data and Devices*, 1st ed., Wiley-IEEE Press, 2015. ISBN: 978-1118640500. DOI: 10.1002/9781118705773. 2

[93] Inoue, H., Adelstein, F., and Joyce, R. A. Visualization in testing a volatile memory forensic tool. In *Proc. of the 11th Annual Digital Forensic Research Conference. DFRWS*, 2011, pp. S42–S51. DOI: 10.1016/j.diin.2011.05.006. 66

[94] Institute, N. F. Hansken, 2016. `https://www.forensicinstitute.nl/products_an d_services/forensic_products/hansken.aspx` 117

[95] Jeon, S., Bang, J., Byun, K., and Lee, S. A recovery method of deleted record for sqlite database. *Personal and Ubiquitous Computing 16*, 6, 2012, pp. 707–715. DOI: 10.1007/s00779-011-0428-7. 81

[96] Josefsson, S. The base16, base32, and base64 data encodings, 2006. RFC 4648. DOI: 10.17487/rfc3548. 39, 58, 105

[97] Karresand, M. and Shahmehri, N. File type identification of data fragments by their binary structure. In *IEEE Information Assurance Workshop*, 2006, pp. 140–147. DOI: 10.1109/iaw.2006.1652088. 60

[98] Karresand, M. and Shahmehri, N. Oscar—file type identification of binary data in disk clusters and ram pages. In *Security and Privacy in Dynamic Environments*. Springer, 2006, pp. 413–424. DOI: 10.1007/0-387-33406-8_35. 60

[99] Kendall, K. and Kornblum, J. Foremost, 2010. `http://foremost.sourceforge.net/` 55

[100] Kent, K., Chevalier, S., Grance, T., and Dang, H. Guide to integrating forensic techniques into incident response. NIST Special Publication 800-86, DOI: 10.6028/nist.sp.800-86. 11, 31, 74

[101] King, C. and Vidas, T. Empirical analysis of solid state disk data retention when used with contemporary operating systems. In *Proc. of the 11th Annual DFRWS Conference. DFRWS'11.*, 2011, pp. S111–S117. DOI: 10.1016/j.diin.2011.05.013. 57, 85

[102] Klein, G., Moon, B., and Hoffman, R. Making sense of sensemaking 1: Alternative perspectives. *IEEE Intelligent Systems 21*, 4, 2006, pp. 70–73. DOI: 10.1109/mis.2006.75. 26

[103] Kornblum, J. Identifying almost identical files using context triggered piecewise hashing. In *The Proc. of the 6th Annual Digital Forensic Research Conference (DFRWS)*, 2006, pp. S91–S97. DOI: 10.1016/j.diin.2006.06.015. 104, 105

[104] Kornblum, J., Medico, A., Cordovano, R., Lowe, J., and Levendoski, M. dcfldd, 2015. http://sourceforge.net/projects/dc3dd/ 32

[105] Lamport, L. Time, clocks, and the ordering of events in a distributed system. *Communications of ACM 21*, 7, July 1978, pp. 558–565. DOI: 10.1145/359545.359563. 66

[106] Leach, P., Mealling, M., and Salz, R. A universally unique identifier (uuid) urn namespace, 2005. RFC 4122. DOI: 10.17487/rfc4122. 36

[107] Li, W.-J., Wang, K., Stolfo, S., and Herzog, B. Fileprints: Identifying file types by n-gram analysis. In *Proc. from the 6th Annual IEEE SMC Information Assurance Workshop, 2005.*, 2005, pp. 64–71. DOI: 10.1109/iaw.2005.1495935. 59

[108] Ligh, M. H., Case, A., Levy, J., and Walters, A. *The Art of Memory Forensics: Detecting Malware and Threats in Windows, Linux, and Mac Memory*, 1st ed., Wiley, 2014. ISBN: 978-1118825099. 2

[109] Lineberry, A. Malicious code injection via /dev/mem. In *BlackHat Europe*, 2009. https://www.blackhat.com/presentations/bh-europe-09/Lineberry/Bl ackHat-Europe-2009-Lineberry-code-injection-via-dev-mem.pdf 65

[110] Lu, R., Lin, X., Liang, X., and Shen, X. S. Secure provenance: The essential of bread and butter of data forensics in cloud computing. In *Proc. of the 5th ACM Symposium on Information, Computer and Communications Security*, 2010, pp. 282–292. DOI: 10.1145/1755688.1755723. 88

[111] Machek, P. Network block device. http://nbd.sourceforge.net/ 55

[112] Manber, U. Finding similar files in a large file system. In *Proc. of the USENIX Winter 1994 Technical Conference*, 1994, pp. 1–10. https://www.usenix.org/legacy/publicatio ns/library/proceedings/sf94/full_papers/manber.finding 105

[113] Martini, B. and Choo, K.-K. R. Cloud storage forensics: Owncloud as a case study. *Journal of Digital Investigation 10*, 4, 2013, pp. 287–299. DOI: 10.1016/j.diin.2013.08.005. 82

[114] Marziale, L., Richard, G., and Roussev, V. Massive threading: Using gpus to increase the performance of digital forensics tools. In *Proc. of the 2007 DFRWS Conference*, 2007, pp. S73–S81. DOI: 10.1016/j.diin.2007.06.014. 55

[115] Mattern, F.   Virtual time and global states of distributed systems.   In *Proc. of the Workshop on Parallel and Distributed Algorithms*, 1988, North-Holland, pp. 120–134. `http://citeseerx.ist.psu.edu/viewdoc/download?doi=10.1.1.63.4399&rep=rep1&type=pdf` 66

[116] Mell, P. and Grance, T. The NIST definition of cloud computing. NIST Special Publication 800-145, DOI: 10.6028/nist.sp.800-145. 82, 85

[117] Metz, J. libewf wiki: Mounting an EWF image. `https://github.com/libyal/libewf/wiki/Mounting` 95

[118] Metz, J.   Expert witness compression format version 2 specification, 2012.   Working draft. `https://github.com/libyal/libewf/blob/master/documentation/Expert%20Witness%20Compression%20Format%202%20(EWF2).asciidoc` 34

[119] Metz, J.   Expert witness compression format specification, 2013.   Working draft. `https://github.com/libyal/libewf/blob/master/documentation/Expert%20Witness%20Compression%20Format%20(EWF).asciidoc` 34, 71

[120] Metz, J. libewf, 2015. `https://github.com/libyal/libewf` 34

[121] Microsoft. Object linking and embedding (OLE) data structures, 2012. `http://csrc.nist.gov/publications/drafts/nistir-8006/draft_nistir_8006.pdf` 55, 106

[122] Monga, V. and Evans, B. L.   Perceptual image hashing via feature points: Performance evaluation and tradeoffs.   *IEEE Transactions on Image Processing 15*, 11, Nov 2006, pp. 3452–3465. DOI: 10.1109/tip.2006.881948. 104

[123] Moulton, S. Re-animating drives and advanced data recovery, 2007. `https://www.defcon.org/images/defcon-15/dc15-presentations/Moulton/Whitepaper/dc-15-moulton-WP.pdf` 30

[124] Muthitacharoen, A., Chen, B., and Mazières, D. A low-bandwidth network file system. In *Proc. of the 18th ACM Symposium on Operating Systems Principles*, 2001, pp. 174–187. DOI: 10.1145/502034.502052. 105

[125] Na, G.-H., Shim, K.-S., Moon, K.-W., Kong, S., Kim, E.-S., and Lee, J. Frame-based recovery of corrupted video files using video codec specifications. *IEEE Transactions on Image Processing 23*, 2, 2014, pp. 517–526. DOI: 10.1109/tip.2013.2285625. 56

[126] National Institute of Justice. Electronic crime scene investigation: A guide for first responders, 2001. `https://www.ncjrs.gov/pdffiles1/nij/187736.pdf` 10

[127] Nelson, A. *Advances in Digital Forensics VIII*.   Springer, 2012, ch. XML Conversion of the Windows Registry for Forensic Processing and Distribution, pp. 51–65. DOI: 10.1007/978-3-642-33962-2. 16

[128] NIST. Computer forensic tool testing program, 2015. `http://www.cftt.nist.gov/` 33

[129] NIST. Computer forensic tool testing program: Disk imaging, 2015. `http://www.cftt.nist.gov/disk_imaging.htm` 33

[130] NIST. Computer forensic tool testing program: Write blockers (hardware), 2015. `http://www.cftt.nist.gov/hardware_write_block.htm` 33

[131] NIST. SHA-3 standard: Permutation-based hash and extendable-output functions, 2015. DOI: 10.6028/nist.fips.202. 99

[132] NIST. National software reference library, 2016. `http://www.nsrl.nist.gov/` 100

[133] NIST Cloud Computing Forensic Science Working Group. NIST Cloud computing forensic science challenges, 2014. (Draft NISTIR 8006). `csrc.nist.gov/publications/drafts/nistir-8006/draft_nistir_8006.pdf`. 85, 120

[134] Oh, J., Lee, S., and Lee, S. Advanced evidence collection and analysis of web browser activity. In *The Proc. of the 11th Annual {DFRWS} Conference 11th Annual Digital Forensics Research Conference*, 2011, pp. S62–S70. DOI: 10.1016/j.diin.2011.05.008. 80

[135] Özer, H., Sankur, B., Memon, N., and Anarim, E. Perceptual audio hashing functions. *EURASIP J. Appl. Signal Process. 2005*, Jan. 2005, pp. 1780–1793. DOI: 10.1155/asp.2005.1780. 104

[136] Palmer, G. A road map for digital forensic research, report from the first digital forensic research workshop (dfrws), 2001. `https://www.dfrws.org/2001/dfrws-rm-final.pdf` 10

[137] Parsonage, H. Computer forensics case assessment and triage, 2009. `http://computerforensics.parsonage.co.uk/triage/ComputerForensicsCaseAssessmentAndTriageDiscussionPaper.pdf` 77

[138] Patterson, E., Roth, E., and Woods, D. Predicting vulnerabilities in computer-supported inferential analysis under data overload. *Cognition, Technology and Work 3*, 4, 2001, pp. 224–237. DOI: 10.1007/s10111-001-8004-y. 26

[139] Penrose, P., Macfarlane, R., and Buchanan, W. Approaches to the classification of high entropy file fragments. *Journal of Digital Investigation 10*, 4, 2013, pp. 372–384. DOI: 10.1016/j.diin.2013.08.004. 61

[140] Pilli, E. S., Joshi, R., and Niyogi, R. Network forensic frameworks: Survey and research challenges. *Journal of Digital Investigation 7*, 1–2, 2010, pp. 14–27. DOI: 10.1016/j.diin.2010.02.003. 71

[141] Pirolli, P. *Information Foraging Theory: Adaptive Interaction with Information.* Oxford University Press, 2009. ISBN: 978-0195387797. 26

[142] Pirolli, P. and Card, S. Sensemaking processes of intelligence analysts and possible leverage points as identified through cognitive task analysis. In *Proc. of the 2005 International Conference on Intelligence Analysis*, 2005. http://researchgate.net/publication/215439203 23

[143] PKWARE Inc. APPNOTE.TXT—.ZIP file format specification, 2014. Version: 6.3.4 https://pkware.cachefly.net/webdocs/casestudies/APPNOTE.TXT 36

[144] Quick, D. and Choo, K.-K. R. Google drive: Forensic analysis of data remnants. *Journal of Network and Computer Applications 40*, April 2014, pp. 179–193. DOI: 10.1016/j.jnca.2013.09.016. 82

[145] Quick, D. and Choo, K. R. Dropbox analysis: Data remnants on user machines. *Journal of Digital Investigation 10*, June 2013, pp. 3–18. DOI: 10.1016/j.diin.2013.02.003. 82

[146] Rabin, M. Fingerprinting by random polynomials, 1981. Technical report 15-81, Harvard University. 105

[147] Ranum, M. Network forensics: Network traffic monitoring, 1997. 70

[148] Ranum, M. J., Landfield, K., Stolarchuk, M., Sienkiewicz, M., Lambeth, A., and Wall, E. Implementing a generalized tool for network monitoring. *Information Security Technical Report 3*, 4, 1998, pp. 53–64. DOI: 10.1016/s1363-4127(99)80034-x. 70

[149] Richard, G. and Roussev, V. Scalpel: A frugal, high performance file carver. In *Proc. of the 2005 DFRWS Conference (DFRWS)*, 2005. https://www.dfrws.org/2005/proceedings/richard_scalpel.pdf 55, 85

[150] Richard, G. and Roussev, V. Next-generation digital forensics. *Communications of the ACM 49*, 2, Feb 2006, pp. 76–80. DOI: 10.1145/1113034.1113074. 117

[151] Richard, G., Roussev, V., and Marziale, L. In-place file carving. In *Research Advances in Digital Forensics III*, P. Craiger and S. Shenoi, Eds. Springer, 2007, pp. 217–230. DOI: 10.1007/978-0-387-73742-3. 55, 95

[152] Rosen, A. ASR expert witness compression format specification. Archived: Oct 10, 2002. 33, 71

[153] Roussev, V. Building a better similarity trap with statistically improbable features. In *42nd Hawaii International Conference on System Sciences*, Jan 2009, pp. 1–10. DOI: 10.1109/hicss.2009.97. 107

[154] Roussev, V. Hashing and data fingerprinting in digital forensics. *IEEE Security Privacy 7*, 2, March 2009, pp. 49–55. DOI: 10.1109/msp.2009.40. 11

[155] Roussev, V. Data fingerprinting with similarity digests. In *Research Advances in Digital Forensics VI*, S. S. Kam-Pui Chow, Ed. Springer, 2010, pp. 207–226. DOI: 10.1007/978-3-642-15506-2. 104, 108

[156] Roussev, V. Building open and scalable digital forensic tools. In *2011 IEEE 6th International Workshop on Systematic Approaches to Digital Forensic Engineering (SADFE)*, May 2011, pp. 1–6. DOI: 10.1109/sadfe.2011.3. 117

[157] Roussev, V. An evaluation of forensics similarity hashes. In *Proc. of the 11th Annual Digital Forensic Research Conference (DFRWS)*, Aug 2011, pp. S34–S41. DOI: 10.1016/j.diin.2011.05.005. 107, 109

[158] Roussev, V. Managing terabyte scale investigations with similarity digests. In *Research Advances in Digital Forensics VIII*, S. S. Gilbert Peterson, Ed. Springer, 2012, pp. 19–34. DOI: 10.1007/978-3-642-33962-2. 108, 109

[159] Roussev, V., Ahmed, I., Barreto, A., McCulley, S., and Shanmughan, V. Cloud forensics—tool development studies and future outlook. *Journal of Digital Investigation*, 2016. DOI: 10.1016/j.diin.2016.05.001. 85, 94

[160] Roussev, V., Ahmed, I., and Sires, T. Image-based kernel fingerprinting. In *Proc. of the 14th Annual Digital Forensic Research Conference (DFRWS)*, Aug 2014, pp. S13–S21. DOI: 10.1016/j.diin.2014.05.013. 101

[161] Roussev, V., Barreto, A., and Ahmed, I. Api-based forensic acquisition of cloud drives. In *Research Advances in Digital Forensics XII*, G. Peterson and S. Shenoi, Eds. Springer, 2016, pp. 213–235. DOI: 10.1007/978-3-319-46279-0. 85, 90, 91, 92, 120

[162] Roussev, V. and Garfinkel, S. File fragment classification-the case for specialized approaches. In *4th International IEEE Workshop on Systematic Approaches to Digital Forensic Engineering, 2009. SADFE '09.*, 2009, pp. 3–14. DOI: 10.1109/sadfe.2009.21. 60

[163] Roussev, V. and McCulley, S. Forensic analysis of cloud-native artifacts. In *Proc. of the 3rd Annual DFRWS Europe (DFRWS-EU)*, 2016, pp. S104–S113. DOI: 10.1016/j.diin.2016.01.013. 85, 110, 111, 113

[164] Roussev, V. and Quates, C. File fragment encoding classification—an empirical approach. In *Proc. of the 13th Annual Digital Forensic Research Conference. DFRWS'13.*, 2013, pp. S69–S77. DOI: 10.1016/j.diin.2013.06.008. 58, 61

[165] Roussev, V., Quates, C., and Martell, R. Real-time digital forensics and triage. *Digital Investigation 10*, 2, 2013, pp. 158–167. DOI: 10.1016/j.diin.2013.02.001. 75, 76, 78

[166] Roussev, V. and Richard, G.   Breaking the performance wall: The case for distributed digital forensics.   In *Proc. of the 2004 Digital Forensic Reasearch Workshop*, 1994. http://citeseerx.ist.psu.edu/viewdoc/download?doi=10.1.1.115.8692&rep=rep1&type=pdf 117

[167] Rowe, N. and Garfinkel, S. Global analysis of drive file times. In *5th IEEE International Workshop on Systematic Approaches to Digital Forensic Engineering (SADFE)*, 2010, pp. 97–108. DOI: 10.1109/sadfe.2010.21. 16

[168] Ruan, K., Carthy, J., Kechadi, T., and Baggili, I. Cloud forensics definitions and critical criteria for cloud forensic capability: An overview of survey results. *Journal of Digital Investigation 10*, 1, 2013, pp. 34–43. DOI: 10.1016/j.diin.2013.02.004. 84

[169] Ruan, K., Carthy, J., Kechadi, T., and Crosbie, M. *Advances in Digital Forensics VII*. Springer, 2011, ch. Cloud Forensics, pp. 35–46. DOI: 10.1007/978-3-642-24212-0. 84

[170] Ruff, N. and Suiche, M. Enter sandman. In *PacSec Applied Security Conference*, 2007. http://www.msuiche.net/pres/PacSec07-slides-0.4.pdf 65

[171] Rukhin, A., Soto, J., Nechvatal, J., Barker, E., Leigh, S., Levenson, M., Banks, D., Heckert, A., Dray, J., and Vo, S. Statistical test suite for random and pseudorandom number generators for cryptographic applications, nist special publication. NIST Special Publication 800-22, Rev 1a, http://csrc.nist.gov/publications/nistpubs/800-22-rev1a/SP800-22rev1a.pdf DOI: 10.6028/nist.sp.800-22. 61

[172] Russinovich, M. and Solomon, D. *Windows Internals*, 5th ed., Microsoft Press, 2009. ISBN: 978-0735625303. 70

[173] Rutkowska, J. Beyond the cpu: Defeating hardware based ram acquisition (part i: Amd case). In *BlackHat USA*, 2007. https://www.blackhat.com/presentations/bh-dc-07/Rutkowska/Presentation/bh-dc-07-Rutkowska-up.pdf 65

[174] Schatz, B. Bodysnatcher: Towards reliable volatile memory acquisition by software. In *Proc. of the 7th Annual Digital Forensic Research Conference. DFRWS*, 2007, pp. S126–S134. DOI: 10.1016/j.diin.2007.06.009. 65, 66

[175] Schatz, B. Wirespeed: Extending the {AFF4} forensic container format for scalable acquisition and live analysis. In *Proc. of the 15th Annual Digital Forensic Research Conference (DFRWS)*, 2015, pp. S45–S54. DOI: 10.1016/j.diin.2015.05.016. 39

[176] Sencar, H. and Memon, N. Identification and recovery of JPEG files with missing fragments. In *Proc. of the 7th Annual Digital Forensic Research Conference. DFRWS*, 2009, pp. S88–S98. DOI: 10.1016/j.diin.2009.06.007. 55

[177] Sollins, K. and Masinter, L. Functional requirements for uniform resource names, 1994. RFC 1737. DOI: 10.17487/rfc1737. 36

[178] Solomon, J., Huebner, E., Bem, D., and Szezynska, M. User data persistence in physical memory. *Journal of Digital Investigation 4*, 2, 2007, pp. 68–72. DOI: 10.1016/j.diin.2007.03.002. 62

[179] Stenberg, D. libcurl—the multiprotocol file transfer library. `https://curl.haxx.se/libcurl/` 38

[180] Stevens, C. Formatting, cloning and duplicating advanced format media, 2011. Technical Paper, Revision 1.0. `http://idema.org/wp-content/plugins/download-monitor/download.php?id=1220` 39

[181] Stüttgen, J. and Cohen, M. Anti-forensic resilient memory acquisition. In *Proc. of the 13th Annual Digital Forensics Research Conference (DFRWS)*, 2013, pp. S105–S115. DOI: 10.1016/j.diin.2013.06.012. 64, 65

[182] Sylve, J., Case, A., Marziale, L., and Richard, G. G. Acquisition and analysis of volatile memory from Android devices. *Journal of Digital Investigation 8*, 3–4, 2012, pp. 175–184. DOI: 10.1016/j.diin.2011.10.003. 64, 65

[183] T-Mobile. T-Mobile unveils the T-Mobile G1—the first phone powered by Android. `http://www.t-mobile.com/company/PressReleases_Article.aspx?assetName=Prs_Prs_20080923` 7

[184] Taft, E., Pravetz, J., Zilles, S., and Masinter, L. The application/pdf media type, 2004. RFC 3778. DOI: 10.17487/rfc3778. 54

[185] Thomas, J. and Cook, K., Eds. Illuminating the path: The research and development agenda for visual analytics. *IEEE Computer Society*, 2005. `http://vis.pnnl.gov/pdf/RD_Agenda_VisualAnalytics.pdf` 24

[186] U.S. Department of Justice, Office of the Inspector General. Audit of the federal bureau of investigation's philadelphia regional computer forensic laboratory, 2015. `https://oig.justice.gov/reports/2015/a1514.pdf` 73

[187] U.S. Department of Justice, Office of the Inspector General. Audit of the federal bureau of investigation's new jersey regional computer forensic laboratory, 2016. `https://oig.justice.gov/reports/2016/a1611.pdf` 73

[188] van Beek, H., van Eijk, E., van Baar, R., Ugen, M., Bodde, J., and Siemelink, A. Digital forensics as a service: Game on. *Journal of Digital Investigation 15*, 2015, pp. 20–38. DOI: 10.1016/j.diin.2014.03.007. 117

[189] Veenman, C. Statistical disk cluster classification for file carving. In *3rd International Symposium on Information Assurance and Security, 2007. IAS 2007.*, 2007, pp. 393–398. DOI: 10.1109/isias.2007.4299805. 60

[190] Voas, J. Networks of "things," 2016. (NIST Special Publication 800-183). nvlpubs.ni st.gov/nistpubs/SpecialPublications/NIST.SP.800-183.pdf. 122

[191] Vömel, S. and Freiling, F. C. Correctness, atomicity, and integrity: Defining criteria for forensically-sound memory acquisition. *Journal of Digital Investigation 9*, 2, 2012, pp. 125–137. DOI: 10.1016/j.diin.2012.04.005. 66

[192] von Neumann, J. First draft of a report on the edvac. *IEEE Annals of the History of Computing 15*, 4, 1993, pp. 27–75. DOI: 10.1109/85.238389. 29

[193] Walter, C. Kryder's law. *Scientific American 293*, 2, 2005, pp. 32–33. http://www.scient ificamerican.com/article/kryders-law/ DOI: 10.1038/scientificamerican0805-32. 73

[194] Willassen, S. Forensic analysis of mobile phone internal memory. In *Advances in Digital Forensics*. Springer, 2005, pp. 191–204. DOI: 10.1007/0-387-31163-7_16. 29, 31

[195] Wu, B., Xu, M., Zhang, H., Xu, J., Ren, Y., and Zheng, N. *A Recovery Approach for SQLite History Recorders from YAFFS2*. Springer Berlin Heidelberg, 2013, pp. 295–299. DOI: 10.1007/978-3-642-36818-9_30. 81

[196] Zaddach, J., Kurmus, A., Balzarotti, D., Blass, E.-O., Francillon, A., Goodspeed, T., Gupta, M., and Koltsidas, I. Implementation and implications of a stealth hard-drive backdoor. In *Proc. of the 29th Annual Computer Security Applications Conference*, 2013, pp. 279–288. DOI: 10.1145/2523649.2523661. 31, 32

[197] Zawoad, S., Kumar, A., and Hasan, R. SecLaaS: Secure logging-as-a-service for cloud forensics. In *Proc. of the 8th ACM SIGSAC Symposium on Information, Computer and Communications Security*, 2013, pp. 219–230. DOI: 10.1145/2484313.2484342. 87, 89

Author's Biography

VASSIL ROUSSEV

Vassil Roussev is a Professor of Computer Science and the Director of the Cyber Security program at the University of New Orleans. Since 2004, Roussev's primary research area has been digital forensics, with a particular emphasis on performance and scalability issues. He is a member of the NIST Working Group on Approximate Matching, and is a Co-Founder and Director of the DFRWS non-profit organization. DFRWS promotes digital forensic research via its two annual technical conferences, in North America and Europe, and the publication of annual challenges and research data sets.

Vassil Roussev is an Editor of the *Journal of Digital Investigation* and the *Journal of Digital Forensics, Security and Law*, and is the author of over 50 peer reviewed publications in cyber security and digital forensics. He received B.S. and M.S. degrees from Sofia University, as well as M.S. and Ph.D. degrees in Computer Science from the University of North Carolina–Chapel Hill.